THE**COMPLETE**GUIDE**TO**
PLAYINGBLUES**GUITAR**

Book One: Rhythm Guitar

JOSEPH**ALEXANDER**

FUNDAMENTAL**CHANGES**

The Complete Guide to Playing Blues Guitar

Book One - Rhythm Guitar

Published by www.fundamental-changes.com

ISBN: 978-1-911267-86-7

Copyright © 2018 Joseph Alexander

www.fundamental-changes.com

Twitter: **@guitar_joseph**

Over 10,000 fans on Facebook: FundamentalChangesInGuitar

Instagram: **FundamentalChanges**

For over 250 Free Guitar Lessons with Videos Check Out

www.fundamental-changes.com

Contents

Introduction

What does it mean when someone says they play blues guitar?

The sheer variation in musical style within the genre of The Blues is almost immeasurable and it would be impossible to cover everything in just one hundred pages.

The roots of The Blues as a well-documented musical style in popular culture are in the 'spirituals', 'work songs' and 'field hollers' sung by African-Americans in the era of slavery, and in the years that followed emancipation. As a result, The Blues is rich in African-American rhythm, harmony, melody and phrasing. One of the most important melodic structures that retains a strong link to this time is the performance of *call and response*, or 'antiphony', where a musical question is sung, and then answered by different voices.

Since the first recorded reference to The Blues (Antonio Maggio's *I Got The Blues* in 1908), the musical form has grown, spread and evolved into many different sub–genres. From early *Delta* blues, through to *Texas* blues and later contemporary rock, virtually all the music we hear today owes its origin to The Blues.

Chronologies of The Blues are widely available and this is not the place for a history lesson (although Alan Lomax's *Land Where The Blues Began* (1993) is a good place to start). However, it is essential that anyone wishing to study modern blues guitar understands the roots of the language.

While the following list of names may not be to your personal taste, please spend time listening to early performances of The Blues. Some of the recordings are poor, and maybe don't include a guitar, but you should be able to identify elements in these early musical roots that influenced the work of more contemporary guitarists, such as B.B. King, Stevie Ray Vaughan and Robben Ford.

I consider the music of the following early blues musicians to be essential listening:

* *Bessie Smith*

* *Ma Rainey*

* *Big Bill Broonzy*

* *Blind Lemon Jefferson*

* *Charley Patton*

* *Leadbelly*

* *Lonnie Johnson*

* *Robert Johnson*

* *Son House*

As guitar construction improved towards the 1950s, and as guitarists became more proficient at solo lead guitar, many of the household names associated with guitar-based blues found fame. Assisted by the public's easier access to recorded music, performers such as T-Bone Walker, John Lee Hooker, Muddy Waters, Howlin' Wolf and B.B. King helped shape the stylistic sound of guitar blues. Once again, any recordings by these performers and others in the late 1940s – 1960s are essential listening.

While these eras helped to define the sound of blues guitar music, the late 1960s to 1980s were the period during which the modern guitar blues style became the foundation of hard rock. Bands like The Yardbirds and Led Zeppelin, featuring guitarists such as Jeff Beck, Eric Clapton and Jimmy Page, drew influences from the Afro–American performers listed above, and forged blues into the rock music we know today.

Jimi Hendrix's ground-breaking albums *Are You Experienced* and *Axis, Bold as Love* in 1967, along with other albums by Beck, Clapton and Page, created the illusion of the Guitar God in the minds of the public. It is significant that the musical language of all four guitarists, and that of many others, was based heavily around the language of the blues.

In 1983, Stevie Ray Vaughan released *Texas Flood*, which has become a defining example of the Texas Blues Guitar style.

While this is far from a complete history of blues guitar, and there are some notable omissions, I highly recommend Martin Scorsese's masterpiece, *Martin Scorsese Presents: The Blues*, a seven DVD box set of the most important blues figures of the last hundred or so years, to help you learn more about the roots and political struggle of The Blues.

With so much musical diversity in just this one genre, it's hard to know where and *when* to begin. There are, however, many topics that are required knowledge and applicable to most styles of guitar blues.

I'm writing this series of books to help break down the language used in modern guitar blues from about 1950 onwards. This is by no means a chronological study, and to make things manageable the series of books is divided into three parts.

Book One: Rhythm Guitar

While there are relatively few blues chord *structures*, there are a multitude of approaches we can take to embellish this standard harmony. We will also examine common riff patterns and *straight* versus *triplet* feel rhythm guitar playing. You will learn the differences between Major and Minor type blues progressions and many different chord *voicings* to use to add great depth and interest to your playing.

There are chapters dedicated to *turnarounds,* open-string riffs and melodic fills (solo phrases) that help us move smoothly from one chord to another.

We go into considerable depth about how to play rhythm guitar with a singer or other solo instrument, using sparse *shell* voicings or higher register *drop 2* chords.

We even study some common non-12-bar blues forms such at the *8-,* and *16-bar* forms.

The largest section of Book One studies the rhythmic *placement* of chords. The aim is to open your ears to the subtlety of *when,* not *what* you play in the bar. In both triplet (12/8) and even (4/4) time we look at how to play on *any* subdivision of the beat so we can play with subtlety and finesse. You will learn to drop chords into the groove wherever you wish and will learn that one small rhythmic drop can be much more powerful than a whole bar of unfocused chordal filler.

Chord extensions are also tackled. Instead of playing just simple Major chords we will cover Dominant 7, 9 and 13 chords comprehensively, plus look at some great opportunities to use *altered* chords.

All in all, *The Complete Guide to Playing Blues Guitar - Part One* aims to answer every common question about blues rhythm guitar.

Book 2: Melodic Phrasing

This book deals with soloing in much, much more detail.

"Melodic Phrasing" is a new concept in blues guitar soloing: Instead of teaching you hundreds of hard-to-remember blues licks, it teaches you to form your own unique vocabulary from basic building blocks of time and rhythm. The focus is on moving away from lick-based playing and developing your own spontaneous improvisation skills. In this way, you will develop a unique voice on your instrument while mastering the elusive skills of blues guitar phrasing.

Covering, but quickly moving on from the essential 'nuts and bolts' of blues playing (accurate bends, expressive vibrato and glissando), Melodic Phrasing looks in depth at the rhythmic fragments that are at the source of every blues guitar line. By mastering and combining these rhythms you instantly form your own unique blues guitar language and develop your own personal style.

There are extensive chapters on note placement – how to play what you want, exactly when you want. The possibilities become endless when we consider music in this way. You will develop a whole new level of awareness of the subdivisions of the beat and learn to twist the same licks into thousands of different, powerful phrases.

Lick displacement is also covered in minute detail – how to move the same line by 1/4, 1/8th or even 1/16th notes to disguise its origins and make it sound fresh, new and personal. This is one of the big secrets of blues guitar phrasing, especially when used across chord changes.

Much time is spent teaching you to organically develop any lick in a strong, musically creative way. This kind of musical development is at the roots of all blues improvisation and is imperative to developing your own musical voice.

You will also master *question and answer phrasing* and begin to use it as a vehicle to develop your own solos.

Book Three: Beyond Pentatonics

"Beyond Pentatonics" shows you how to break away from the Minor pentatonic soloing rut that many blues guitarists quickly fall into.

The first half of Beyond Pentatonics shows you how to target the most powerful notes from each chord in a blues progression to deliver the greatest emotional effect.

Every chord change is covered in minute detail, with clear diagrams and dozens of great licks to learn. You'll quickly find yourself playing emotive, original solos that you never thought possible.

The second half of Beyond Pentatonics, gives you many possible scale choices for each chord in the blues progression. Essential scale choices are given for the I, IV and V chords, with theory and important concepts clearly explained.

There are over 125 pieces of authentic blues vocabulary, plus many tricks of the trade to help you incorporate these compelling sounds into your solos.

There is no better, more detailed book to teach you the secrets of blues guitar soloing.

These three books are now available in a compilation edition from Amazon.com

Listen carefully, take your time and above all, have fun!

Joseph

Get the Audio

The audio files for this book are available to download for free from **www.fundamental-changes.com** and the link is in the top right corner. Simply select this book title from the drop-down menu and follow the instructions to get the audio.

We recommend that you download the files directly to your computer, not to your tablet, and extract them there before adding them to your media library. You can then put them on your tablet, iPod or burn them to CD. On the download page there is a help PDF and we also provide technical support via the contact form.

Kindle / eReaders

To get the most out of this book, remember that you can double tap any image to enlarge it. Turn off 'column viewing' and hold your kindle in landscape mode.

Chapter One – The Basic 12-bar Blues Structure

As much as it is a cliché and the starting point for a million guitarists, the standard *12-bar blues progression* is essential knowledge for any guitar player. It is the basis of countless songs, and has been in the musician's repertoire for longer than living memory.

We will begin by looking at the most common 12-bar blues form before looking at common alterations, additions, and riffs.

While it is hopefully obvious, the form we are studying is named the 12-bar blues because as a musical structure it is 12-bars long. In its most basic form, it contains just three chords and all of them are taken from the Major scale that you may already know. These chords are formed on the first, fourth and fifth *degrees* (notes) of the Major scale.

For example, in the key of A Major:

A B C# D E F# G#

We use the chords A Major, D Major and E Major.

The degrees of a scale are always described by Roman numerals:

1 = I

4 = IV

5 = V

So, in the key of A Major:

A = I

D = IV and

E = V

When we use Roman numerals to describe scale tones it doesn't matter which key we are in, we can always use them to explain the relationships between chords. In a sense, it is musical algebra because we describe the relationships between chords rather than the chords themselves.

In modern Western music (especially pop, rock and blues), chords I, IV and V are the most commonly used chords in all songs.

The simplest 12-bar blues progression uses just chords I, IV and V. While it might not be the most exciting rendition of The Blues you will ever hear, it is important to know the foundations of the progression before launching into the many possible variations.

Study the following chord chart. I have shown both the letter names and the Roman numeral description of each chord, along with an open position chord voicing so you can play along with the audio example.

Example 1a:

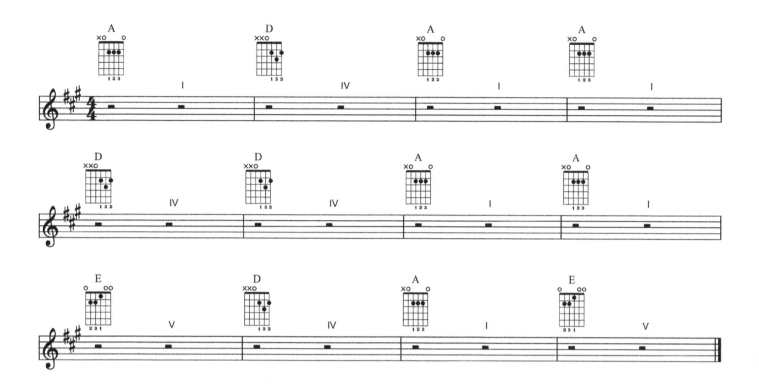

Broadly speaking, there are two main musical feels used in blues rhythm: *straight* (or even) feel and the *swing* (or triplet) feel. The triplet feel is more common and can be heard in famous blues tunes such as Stormy Monday (T-Bone Walker), Blues Power (Albert King), or Five Long Years (Buddy Guy).

The straight blues feel is important and used in many songs, such as Scuttle Buttin' (Stevie Ray Vaughan), Messin' with the Kid (Buddy Guy) and Crying at Daybreak (Howlin' Wolf). It is more common in rock and pop songs than in, what a traditionalist might consider to be, *true* blues. However, the straight blues is an easier place to start.

The first exercise is to play the correct chords just on beat 1 and beat 3.

If you don't understand the notation, listen to the audio examples and try to play along with the recorded versions.

The audio files for this book are available to download for free from **www.fundamental-changes.com** and the link is in the top right corner. Simply select this title from the drop-down menu and follow the instructions to get the audio.

Example 1b:

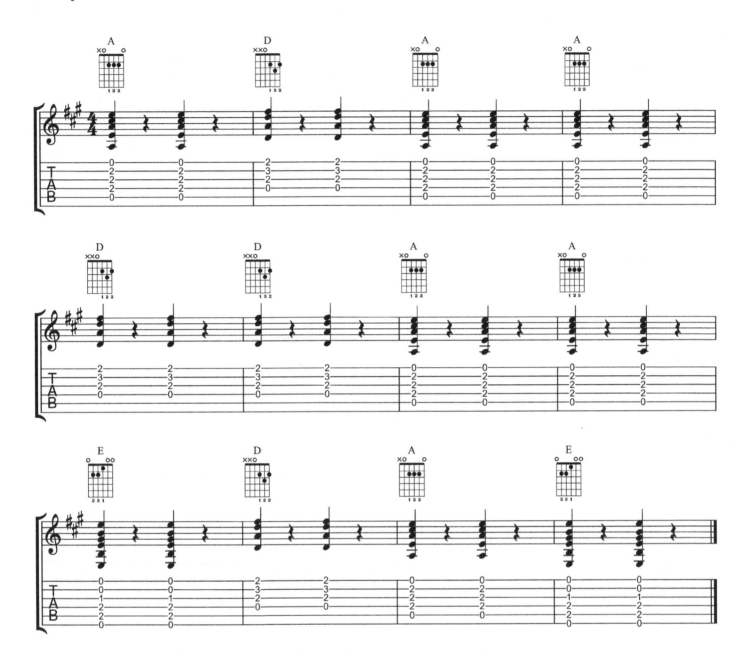

The next exercise is to strum on just beats *2 and 4* as shown in **example 1c:**

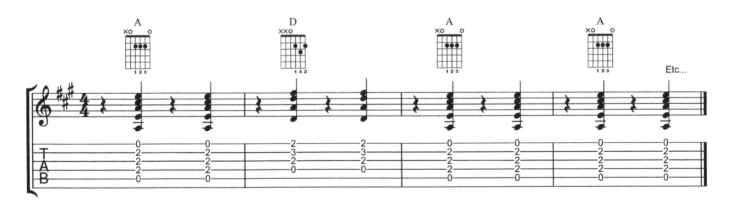

Finally, try adding a bit of a groove to the rhythm guitar by playing on one of the *off-beats* (half way between the main pulses). Listen to the audio track if you're not sure of how this rhythm sounds. In the following example play on beat 1, beat 2 and the off-beat of beat 4. (4&).

Example 1d:

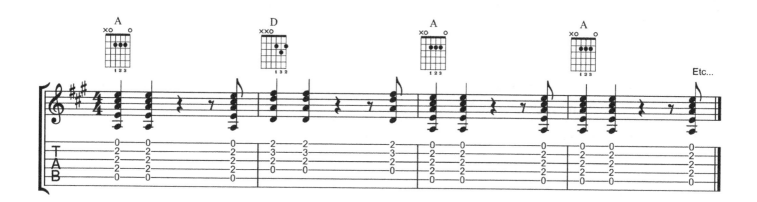

Examples 1a-1d are all examples of a *straight* blues feel. Each beat is divided evenly into two equal halves and this musical feel is found often in rock and pop music. You can count *"1 and 2 and 3 and 4 and"* throughout the progression.

We will look at more ways to subdivide the bar and free up your playing in Chapter Seven, but for now keep jamming along with Backing Track 1 and see if you can find more places to hit the chords. Be led by the groove of the backing track and use the bass and drums to guide you.

The Triplet Blues

The triplet blues has a more laidback, lazy feel at slow tempos, although it can get quite bouncy when we speed things up. Each of the four main beats in the bar is divided into *three* even subdivisions giving a total of twelve quavers (1/8th notes) in a bar. This is what the *time signature* at the start of the following bar of music means: Twelve 1/8th notes in the bar. It is musical convention to group them into threes.

A bar of 12/8 looks like this:

There are plenty of ways to divide a bar of 12/8 and we will explore these in Chapter Eight, but for now let's stick with some of the more popular grooves.

We can still play on beats 1 and 3.

Example 1e:

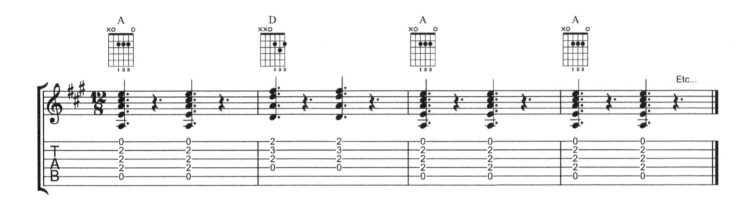

Listen to example 1e before you play it. The rhythmic feel is a bit bouncier so you might find it a little harder to place the chord accurately. Even though you're still playing on beats 1 and 3, the musical feel is very different. This triplet feel is common in blues and R&B.

Now play on just beats 2 and 4.

Example 2f:

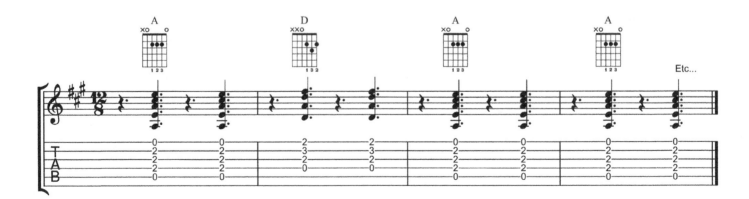

The final 12/8 example (for now) teaches you to play on the *first and third* 1/8th note of each beat. This is one of the most important basic blues rhythm patterns. As always, listen carefully to the audio examples to help you lock in with the musical feel.

Example 1g:

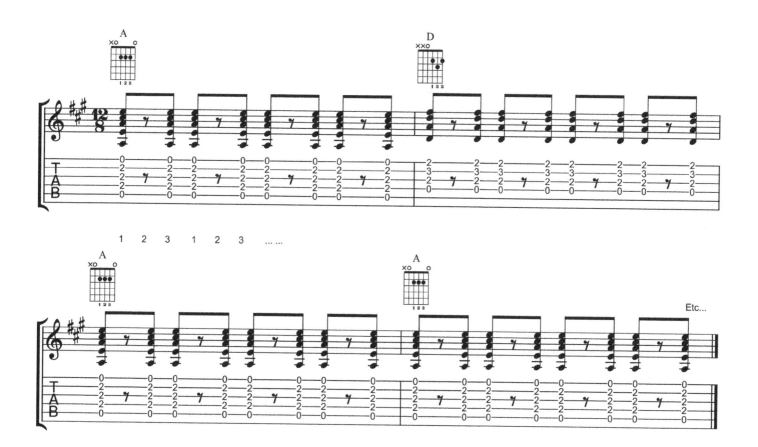

In terms of playing technique, it can be a great help to rest your strumming hand lightly on the strings to produce a muted, choppy sound. This will help to articulate the chords more clearly. You may also wish to let the first note of every beat ring slightly longer to create a less aggressive sound.

Example 1h:

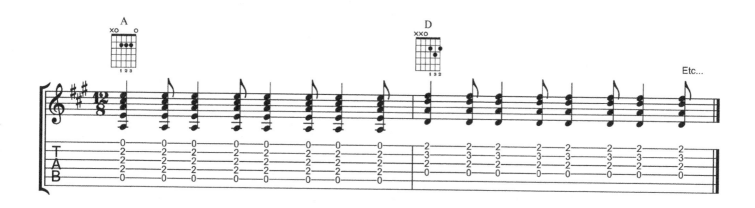

Spend time experimenting with these rhythms and see what you can come up with. Listen again to your favourite blues songs and work out whether they are played in a straight or triplet feel.

The examples in this chapter have all used Major chords. Work through the chapter again but this time substitute each chord for its equivalent '7' chord:

For example, instead of playing A Major, play A7. Here are the chord shapes you will need:

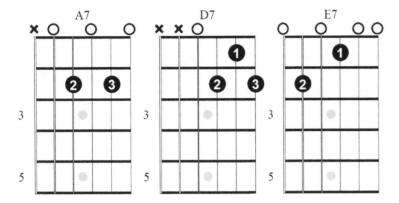

Finally, play the 12-bar blues progression using *Minor* chords:

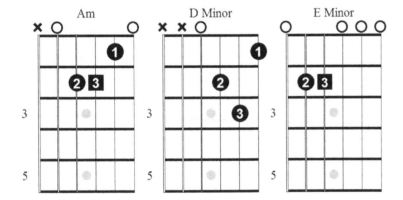

Notice how the *quality* of the chord dramatically effects the mood of the song.

Chapter Two – Open-String Blues Riffs and Variations

While it is essential to know the structure of a 12-bar blues, our rhythm guitar playing will quickly get stagnant if we stick to just playing chords.

It is a common technique to create riffs and open-string bass lines while simultaneously outlining the chord changes, as shown in the previous chapter. In this chapter, we will explore some classic examples of open string guitar riffs.

The following examples are played as *triplet* feel rhythms in the audio examples, however you should experiment by playing them as both straight and triplet feels.

Example 2a is a typical blues riff that can be used anytime there is an A Major chord (Chord I) in the progression. This idea has been used by *every* blues guitarist at some point so you need to learn it. Your picking hand continually strums the bass note (A) on the 5th string *with* a moving note on the 4th string.

Use the 1st and 3rd fingers of your fretting hand to rock backwards and forwards between the alternating notes.

Example 2a:

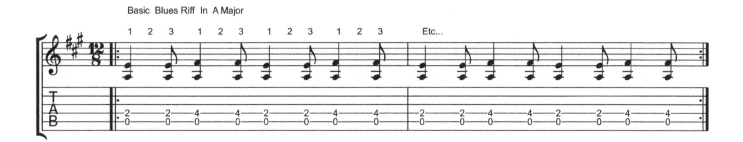

Listen to the audio example and play along with it to internalise the triplet feel. The first strum of each two-note group is longer and the second is shorter.

If we count '1 2 3 1 2 3 1 2 3 1 2 3' through each bar, the first strum lasts for the counts of 1 and 2, and the second strum lasts for just the 3rd count. Count aloud as you play along with each audio example.

To play this blues riff on the D Major chord (chord IV), simply shift the pattern onto the 4th and 3rd strings. We're playing *the same* riff, just moved over one string. Make sure you keep the unplayed bass strings quiet with a bit of palm muting.

Example 2b:

Finally, to play this riff for the E Major chord (chord V) shift this pattern onto the bottom two strings.

Example 2c:

Practise switching between each of the previous three examples. When you're ready, you can use these riffs to play through a whole blues progression.

Example 2d:

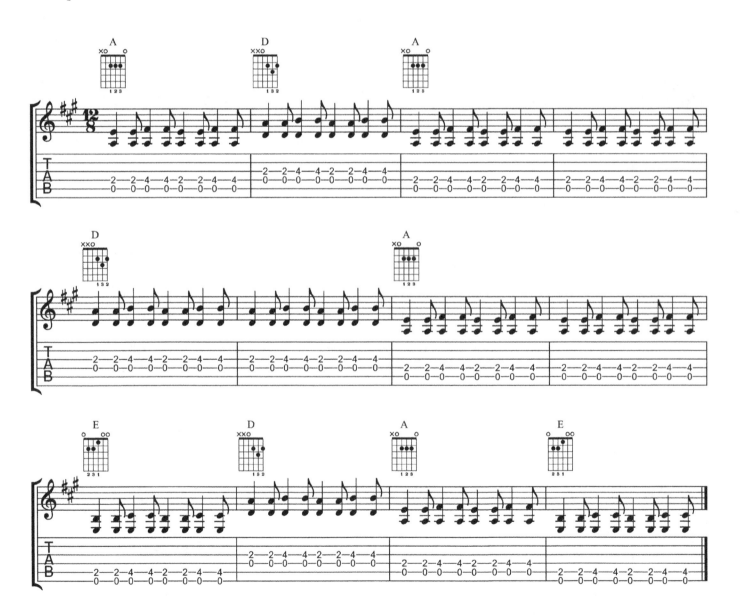

This simple pattern adds great depth to the guitar part when we play blues rhythm and is much more interesting than simply playing chords.

There are variations to the basic pattern that can be inserted anywhere to add even more interest and variation. Subtle variations in the rhythm guitar part can help give the soloist creative ideas and build the groove of the music for both the band and the audience.

In this example use your *little finger* to stretch out and play the 5th fret of the fourth string on beat 3. Move this idea through the chord changes as we did in example 2d.

Example 2e:

The next variation adds a hammer-on idea on the fifth string.

Example 2f:

Again, this riff can be used on the A, D and E chords by simply moving it across string groups as you learned earlier in the chapter.

Another classic riff in the style of John Lee Hooker uses 'pull-offs' to create a descending bass line at the end of each bar.

Example 2g:

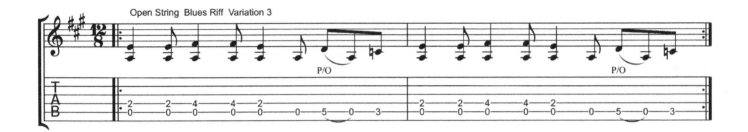

This next example combines previous ideas and uses a bass note on a lower string to give even more movement in the guitar part.

Example 2h:

As always, practise moving this idea through all three chords.

Until now, all the bass fills have taken place on the final few beats of each bar. We can easily shake things up a bit by adding a fill on beat 2.

Example 2i:

A great approach is to split each chord into two parts to *displace* the bass line.

Example 2j:

Once you have a few of these riffs under your fingers, mix and match them in a 12-bar blues progression. All the ideas are freely interchangeable so slot them in wherever you feel they work.

One possible example out of the thousands of permutations is shown below. I've added a couple of new fills to keep you on your toes!

Example 2k:

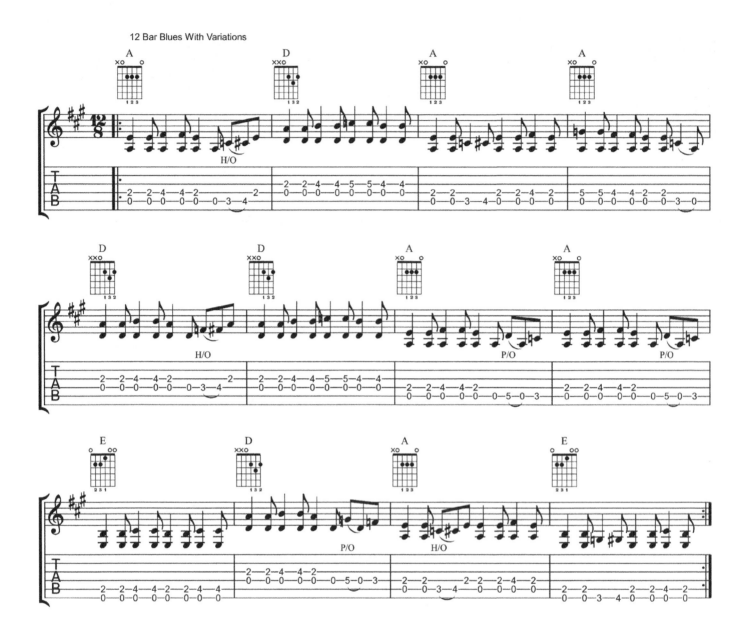

To get inspiration of what can be achieved with this simple rhythm guitar technique, listen to Pride and Joy by Stevie Ray Vaughan. There's only one guitar playing on that intro!

In Pride and Joy, Stevie Ray Vaughan combines the kinds of bass lines we have studied in this chapter with simultaneous chord playing. This hybrid of chords+bassline is typical of the Texas Blues style. Let's look at a few short examples understand this kind of playing.

E Major is normally the most common key for a guitar-based 12-bar blues for many reasons, but one of the main ones is that we can use the open E string to form bass lines as we play chords. Here's one way to add a bass line to an E Major chord in 12/8. Use strict alternate picking on this idea to help you get into the feel of the riff.

Example 2l:

We can also apply this idea to an A Major chord:

Example 2m:

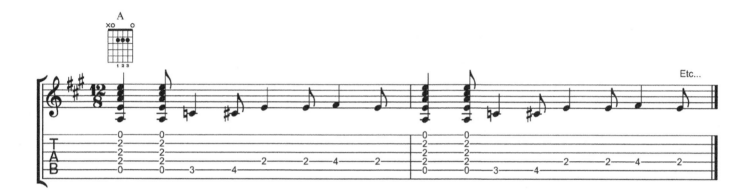

Another reason guitarists like to play in the key of E is that all the open strings are available to play. This is handy when we want to hammer onto a chord from nowhere. With this technique we can play two chords in a bar with the walking bass line.

Example 2n:

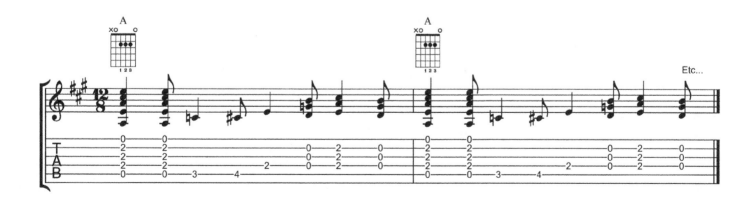

Another approach in this style is to use two different chords in one bar. The next example is heard as a riff in E Major despite the strong A Major chord late in the bar.

Example 2o:

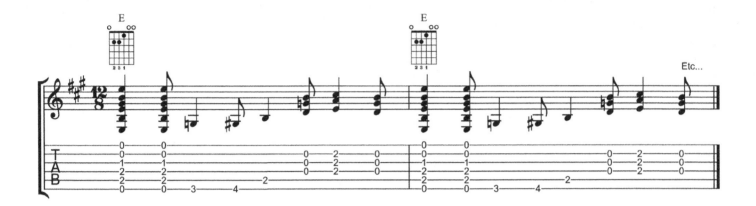

Another great Stevie Ray Vaughan bass line to check out is the one from the track, Rude Mood.

Listening to bass lines can be a great source of ideas to emulate in your playing. Try stealing a few!

It's important to point out that on the turnaround section (the final four bars), the final V chord is often *delayed* by up to two beats. Play through example 2p to learn this important technique in the key of A.

Example 2p:

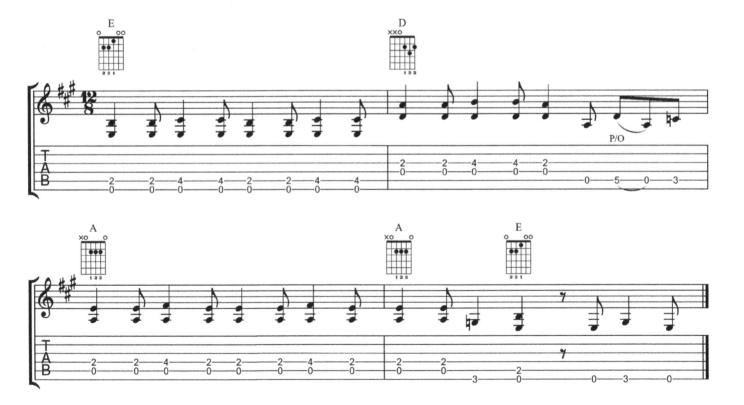

The displacement of the final V chord can occur due to a turnaround lick that starts in on chord I in bar eleven (bar three in the following example). Notice how the lick in the A Major delays the V chord (E).

Example 2q:

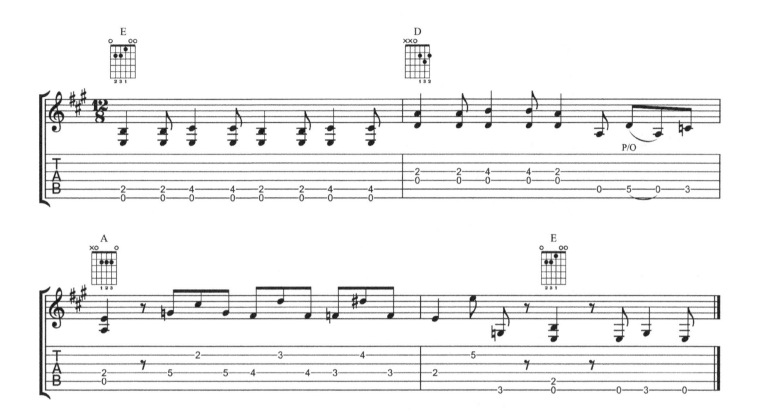

This rhythmic idea happens often in both Texas and Delta blues, so listen out for it.

Chapter Three – Using Dominant 7 Chords

While the 12-bar blues derives from chords I, IV and V in the Major scale, it is common to substitute these Major chords for any other chord quality you wish. The most common substitutions are to use Dominant 7 (7) and Minor 7 (m7) chords.

We briefly covered open position Dominant 7 chords in Chapter One:

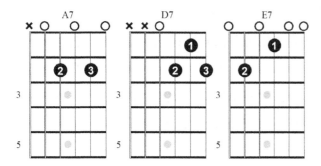

The next example shows how to play the 12-bar blues using Dominant 7 chords instead of Major ones.

Example 3a:

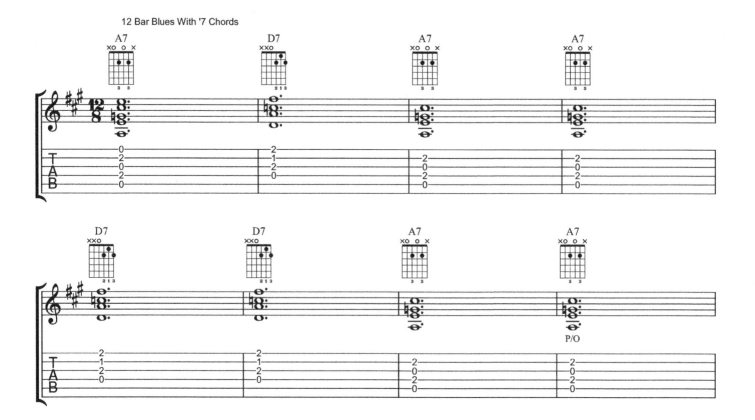

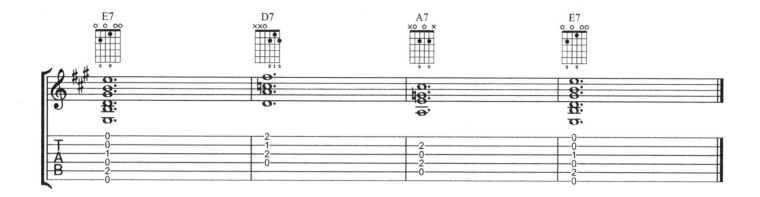

Notice how the whole mood of the music has altered from being happy with Major chords to being a bit more laid back and smooth with the Dominant 7 chords.

All the riffs you learned in the previous chapter work over this progression so try combining the chord and bass line approach we learned in Chapter Two with the Dominant 7 chord approach.

These open position chords are important to know, but to expand our ability to play The Blues in *any* key we need to learn to play *barre* chords.

The first shapes to learn when moving to barre chords are given here,

Example 3b:

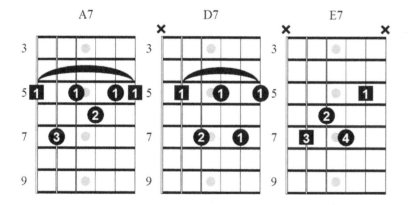

Barre chords are movable chord shapes. Once you have learned a barre chord it can be moved anywhere on the neck to play the same chord *type* with a different bass note. For example, shifting the A7 barre chord shape from the 5th fret to the 7th fret means that the chord becomes B7. Moving a D7 barre down by two frets creates C7 chord.

Replace the chord voicings in example 3a with these barre chord shapes and play through the progression.

Example 3c:

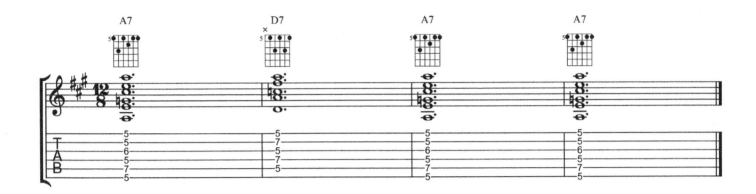

Let's add some rhythmic movement to the 12-bar blues by splitting each barre chord into a bass note and a chord stab to add interest and texture to the rhythm guitar part. Continue the following pattern throughout the 12-bar blues.

Example 3d:

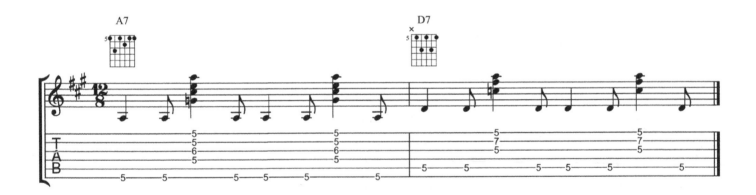

I normally use *palm muting* on the bass notes to give a more percussive effect and then let the chord ring for slightly longer to create a multi-layered texture in the rhythm guitar part. You can hear this idea in the audio example.

A common idea in blues rhythm guitar is to slide into the barre chord from a semitone below. If the slide is done from a weak beat to a strong beat you can always use this technique.

The technical challenge is to make sure that the chord you are sliding from, for example Ab7, rings through into the following A7 chord. The trick is to find just the right amount of pressure that allows you to hold the chord down while sliding it a semitone. The full six-string chord shape is held in every slide, however I normally just strum the top three or four strings.

Use your first finger to play the final note in each bar to help you get into position for the next barre chord. The whole 12-bar progression is played in example 3e, but only the first two bars are notated. Listen carefully and apply these slides to each chord in the progression.

Example 3e:

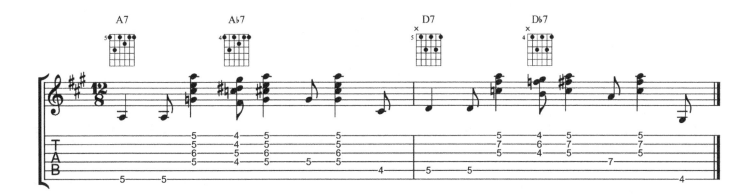

Here is another idea that begins just before beat one.

Example 3f:

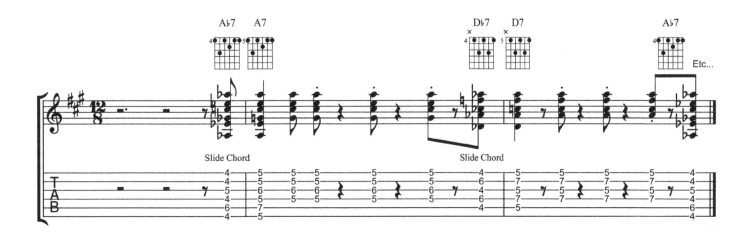

You can also slide two semitones.

Example 3g:

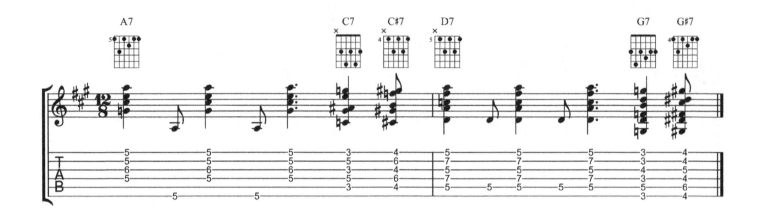

Again, listen carefully to the audio examples to get the feel and placement of these examples.

You can use the same rhythms to approach the target chord from *above*. This idea is notated over the first three bars below.

Example 3h:

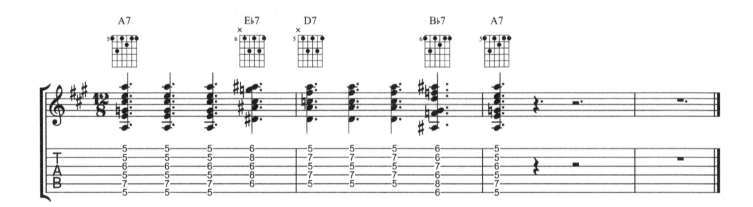

We can apply the earlier open-string riffs to barre chords. Some of the following examples require quite a stretch in the fretting hand, so if you find that you can't reach, try dropping your thumb lower on the back of the neck and remember you don't have to hold *all* the notes in the chord. It is quite acceptable to just play the bottom two strings if the stretch requires it.

Here is the basic blues riff with the A7, D7 and E7 chords.

Example 3i:

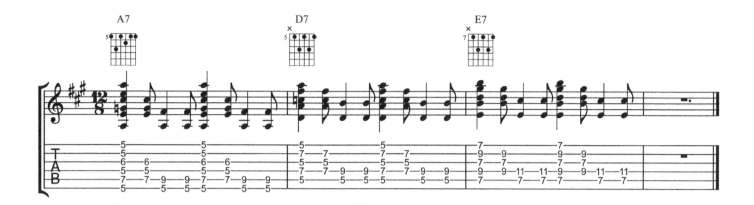

We can use an even bigger stretch with our little finger.

Example 3j:

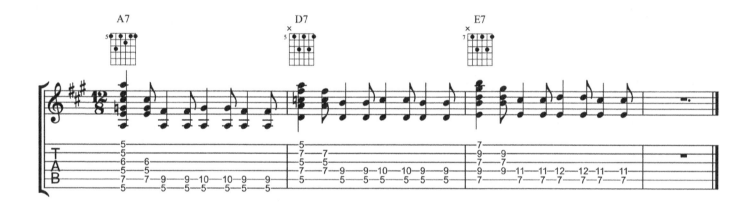

We can even add a sliding chord for extra movement in the rhythm part.

Example 3k:

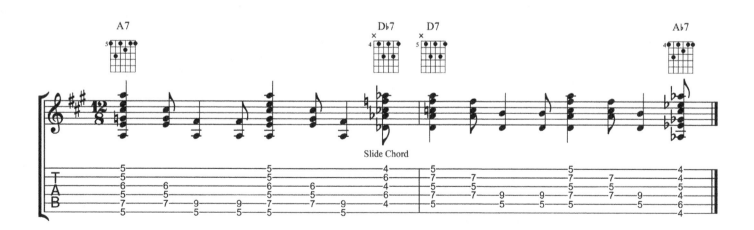

The movement in the rhythm guitar part can be at the top of the chord, not just in the bass. The following examples work well when we play rhythm underneath a guitar solo but can be a little too busy when there is a vocal melody.

In the following examples, use your little finger (pinky) to add a moving melody note at the top of the chord. With my picking hand, I use my thumb to play the bass notes and my index, middle and ring fingers to play the three note block chords.

Example 3l:

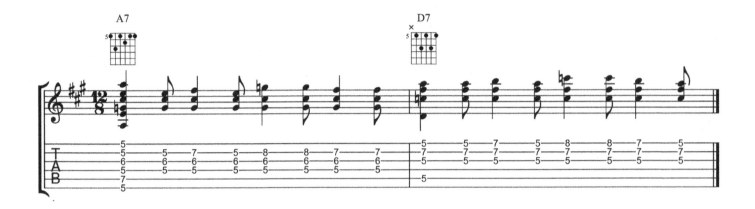

Example 3m:

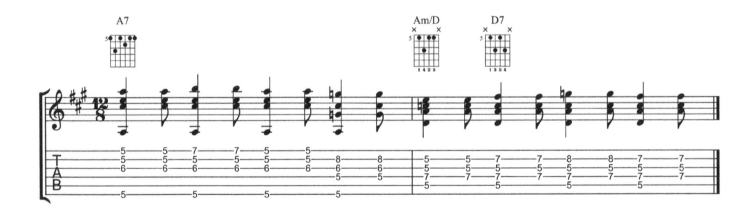

We can find many melodies to give subtle movement to the rhythm guitar part, just by moving our little finger. Ideas like this can give a lot of interest to the song, just be careful not to get in the way of the singer or soloist.

Chapter Four – Extensions to the Dominant 7 Chord

Dominant 7 chords are often used in The Blues, but we can use *any* chord from the Dominant 7 *family*.

This isn't a theory book, so to keep things simple the Dominant chord family includes 7s, 9s, 11s and 13s and these are all normally interchangeable. For example, if you see an A7 written there is often no reason why you can't substitute it for an A9 or A13 chord. You need to be more careful with Dominant 11 chords so we will avoid these for now.

Think of Dominant 9s, 11s and 13s as *extended* Dominant 7 chords. While the basic Dominant chord quality and function are the same, these extensions add depth, colour and interest to our music.

Here are some useful voicings for Dominant 9s and 13s for chords I, IV, and V.

Note that the voicing of A9 here is *rootless*. This works best in the context of a band situation where the bass player plays the root.

Example 4a:

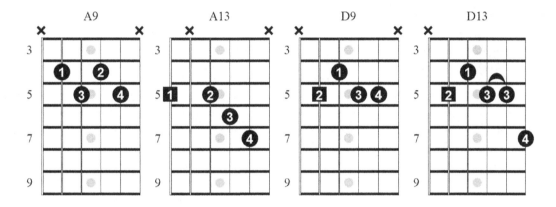

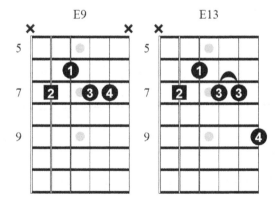

We will begin by substituting some of the original '7' chord voicings in the 12-bar blues with *extended* chord voicings.

Example 4b:

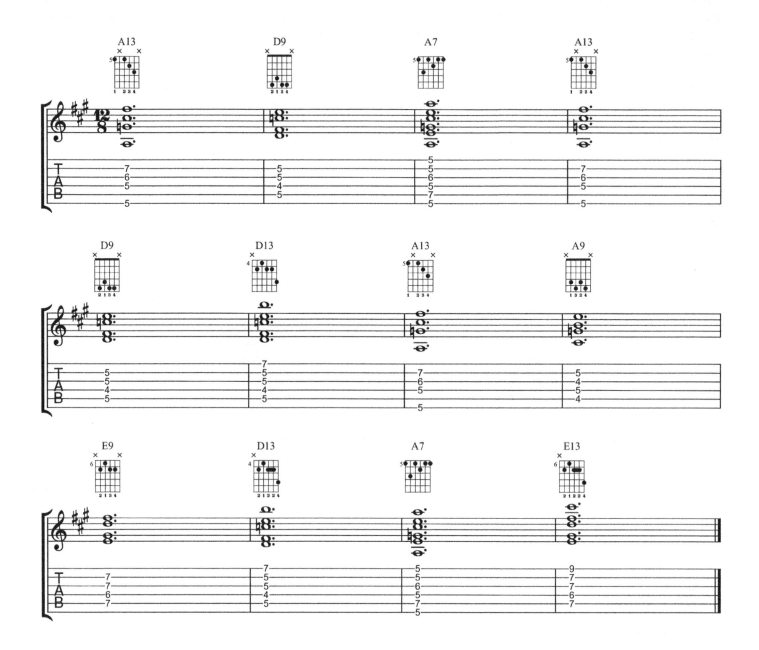

By using the idea of approaching each chord by stepwise movement we can easily generate great interest in the rhythm guitar part.

Study example 4c to hear how this kind of movement decorates the chords in the previous example.

Notice that I freely change between approaching each chord from above *and* below.

Example 4c:

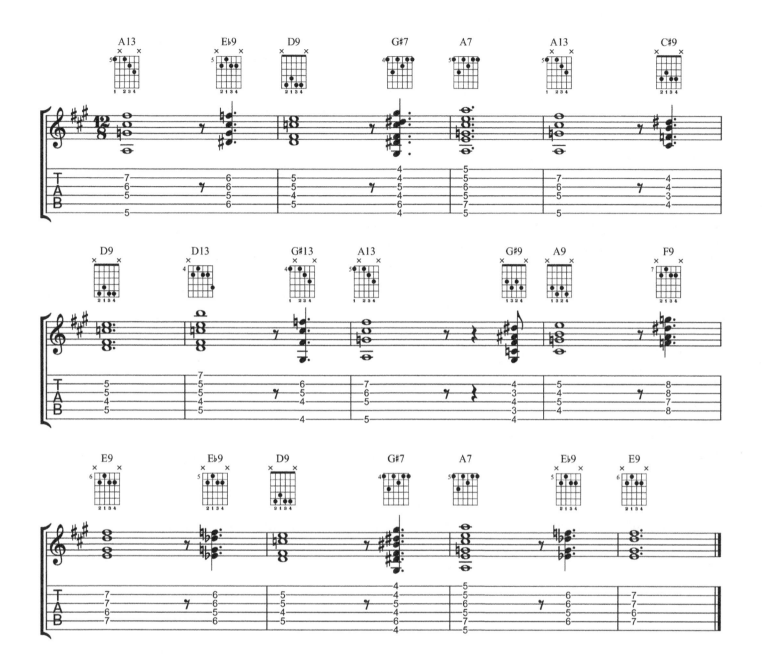

It is acceptable to change between chords from the same family in the same bar. For example, you could play this:

Example 4d:

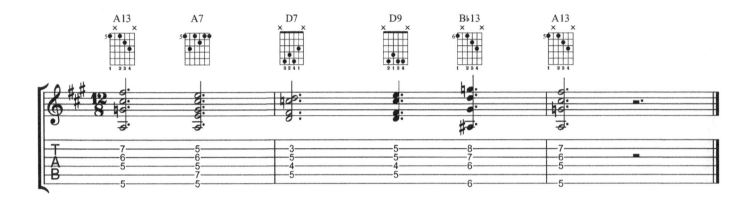

Listen to the melodic movement this creates on the second string and look out for the semitone movement from above in bar two as I approach the A13 with a Bb13.

The key to internalising these chord ideas is to practise rhythm guitar with a backing track. Backing Track 4: Triplet Blues in A, isolates the drum and bass parts so you can provide your own rhythmic accompaniment on the guitar.

Focus on changing smoothly between chords in time, and experimenting with different extensions for each chord. For example, I like to play A13 for chord I and D9 for chord IV, but you may come up with many different combinations.

Practise changing between chord voicings and moving between different extensions of each Dominant chord in each bar. Finally, practise the bass line examples from Chapter Two, and be sure to listen to the bass and drums in the backing track to *lock in* with their feel.

Chapter Five – Common Variations to the 12-Bar Blues

There are many common chord variations that can be used while staying within the 12-bar blues structure. You will find the alterations in this chapter used in hundreds of blues tunes and you will hear them all the time on classic recordings.

Let's add some variations to the first four bars of the tune. A common idea is to go to the (V) chord in the second half of bar three. In example 5a I approach some chords by step, but the thing to notice is the new E9 in bar three. Adding chord V here helps to break up the static two bars of A7 in the original 12-bar blues progression.

Example 5a:

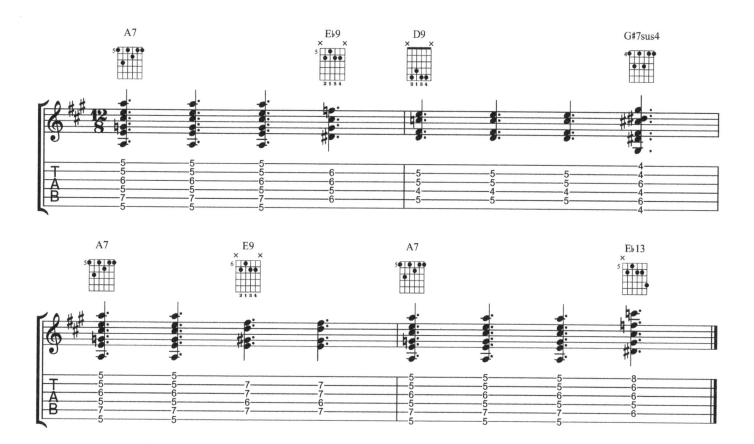

Instead of playing the E9 chord in bar three it is common to hear a Bb7 (A Dominant 7 chord built on the bII of the scale). This is idea is used in T-Bone Walker's Stormy Monday Blues.

Example 5b:

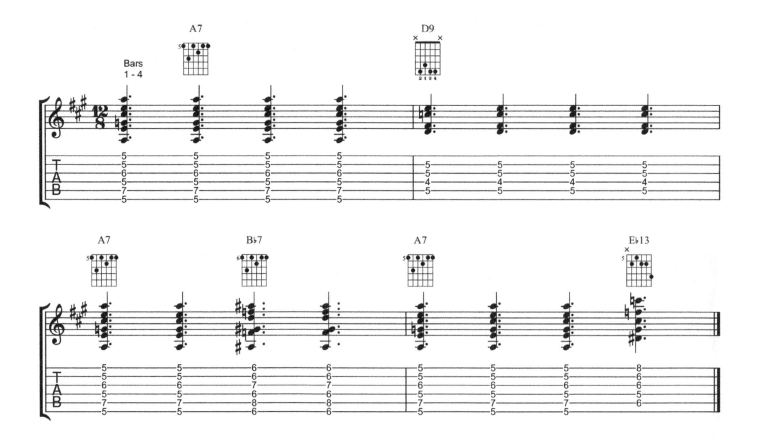

In the 12-bar blues there is another static two-bar section in bars five and six. This time there are two bars of D7 (chord IV).

To add harmonic movement, we can play an Eb diminished 7 chord in bar six. This is an idea borrowed from the jazz blues style and sounds great in a standard 12-bar.

Here is one way to play the Eb Diminished 7 chord:

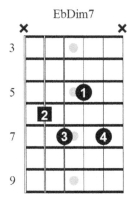

Can you see that this chord is just like a D7 chord that has had the root raised by a semitone?

Example 5c:

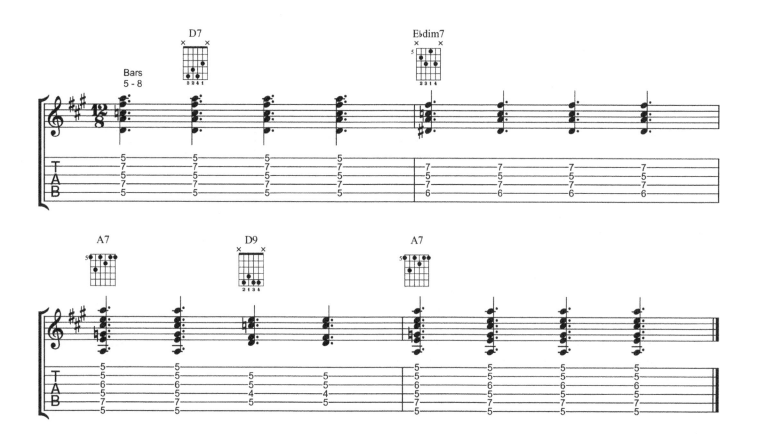

One way to break up the two bars of A7 in bars seven and eight is to add an F#7 (chord VI7) in bar eight. Once again, this idea is borrowed from the jazz repertoire but is often used in a Texas style blues.

Example 5d combines the Eb Diminished 7 chord and the added chord VI into one example. The second four bars of The Blues progression could look like this:

Example 5d:

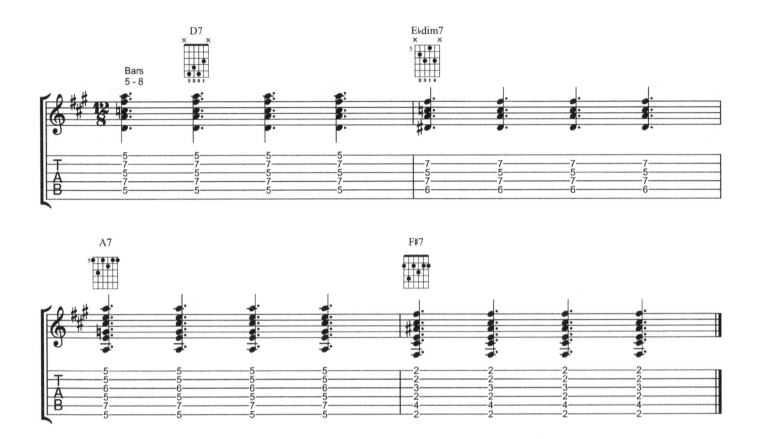

The F#7 can approached by a stepwise movement if you wish.

When we use chord VI (F#7) in bar eight, you can probably hear that the harmony wants to go somewhere different from the usual V chord (E7) that is normally played. The traditional way to follow chord VI in this context is to play chord B Minor 7 (iim7) in bar nine.

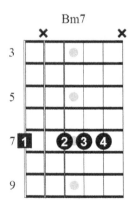

When it occurs in bar 9, the Bm7 delays the appearance of the important Dominant chord by one bar.

Example 5e:

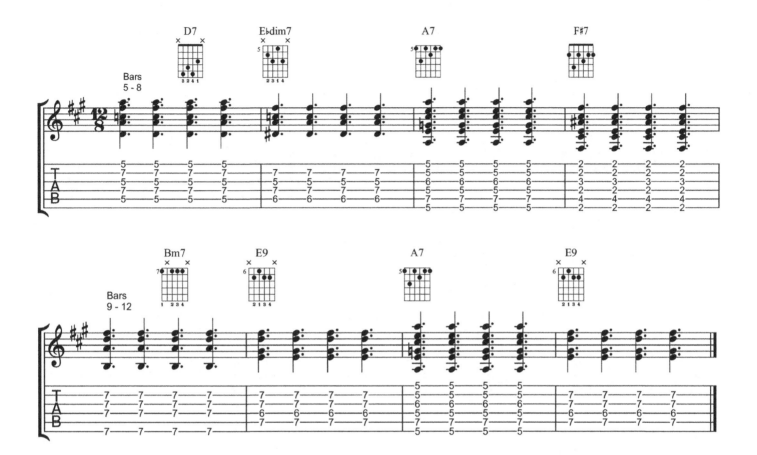

Another great way to delay the E7 (V) that occurs in bar nine is to substitute it for an F7 or F9 (bVI) chord. These are some of the most important variations that occur in the first eight or nine bars of a traditional 12-bar blues progression.

Example 5f:

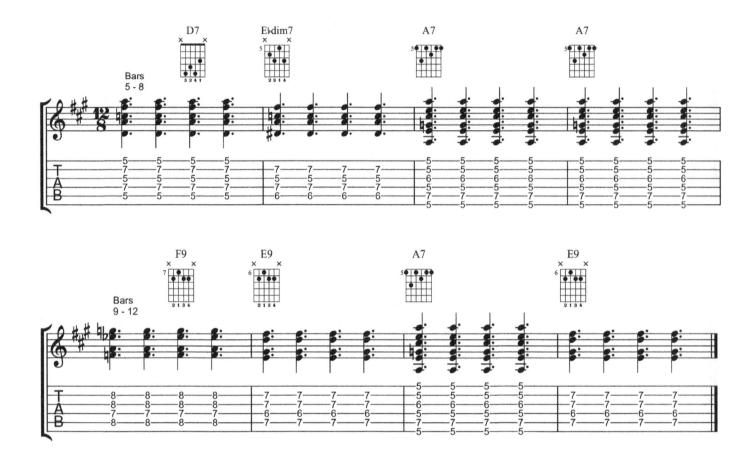

Another way to add movement to bars seven and eight is to apply a chord sequence made famous by T-Bone Walker in Stormy Monday Blues. It's easier to see on paper than it is to explain in words so study the following example.

Example 5g:

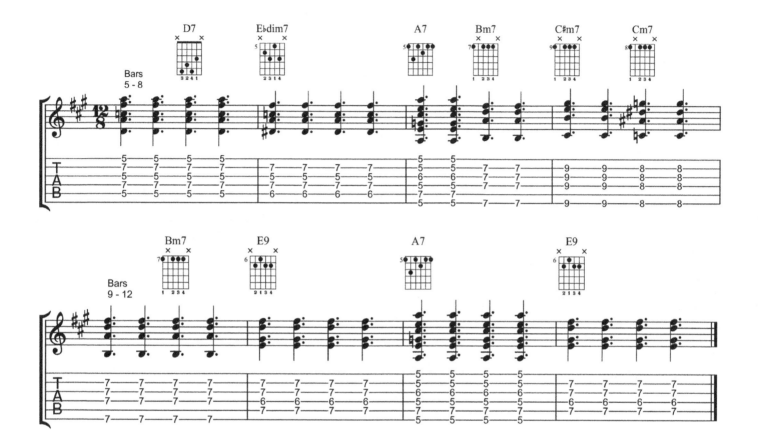

Chapter Six – Blues Turnarounds

The final four-bar section of a 12-bar blues is called the *turnaround* because it is designed to 'turn the song around' back to the beginning of the chord sequence. This is where most of the musical tension in a blues exists, both harmonically and melodically. You will find that *altered* chords are often used in the turnaround section and the *harmonic rhythm* (chord frequency) increases.

To remind yourself of the final four bars of a standard blues, look at the following notation.

Example 6a:

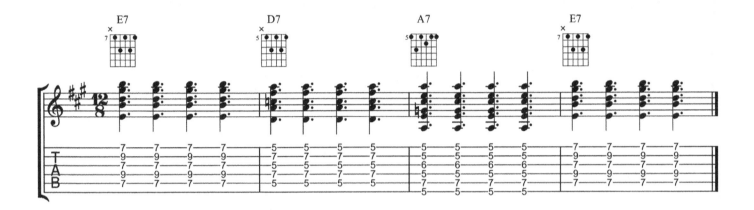

A common variation is to add the subdominant (IV) and tonic (I) chords to the final two-bar section:

Example 6b:

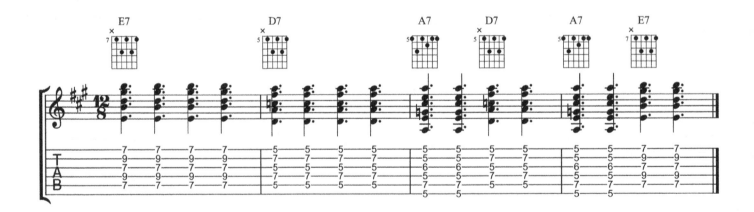

Remember, all these chords are interchangeable with any chord in their Dominant 7 family, i.e., you can play A13s instead of A7s etc.

Another useful variation is to play a bVI (F or F9) chord with the D7 in bar ten.

Example 6c:

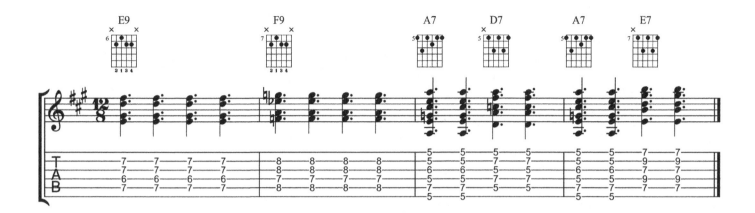

Before looking at the next chord progression go back and remind yourself of example 5e.

When we use chords VI and II in bars eight and nine it is common to repeat the chords from bars eight to ten at double the frequency in the final two bars of the form.

Example 6d:

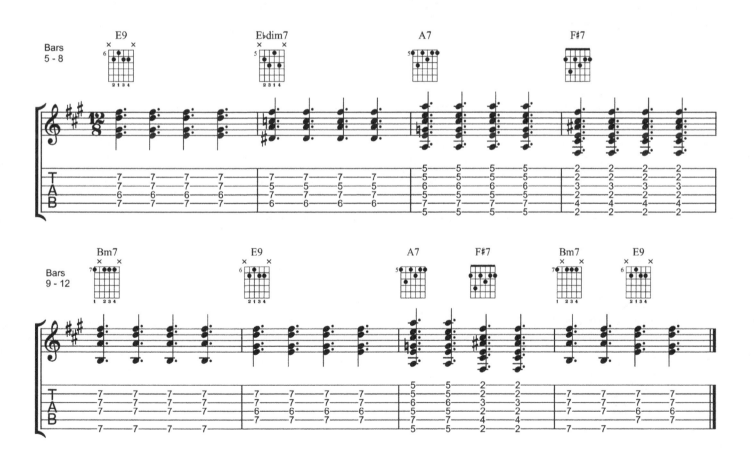

The previous progression is set up by the Eb diminished 7 in bar six although you are by no means obliged to play the whole turnaround if you use the diminished chord.

Example 6e:

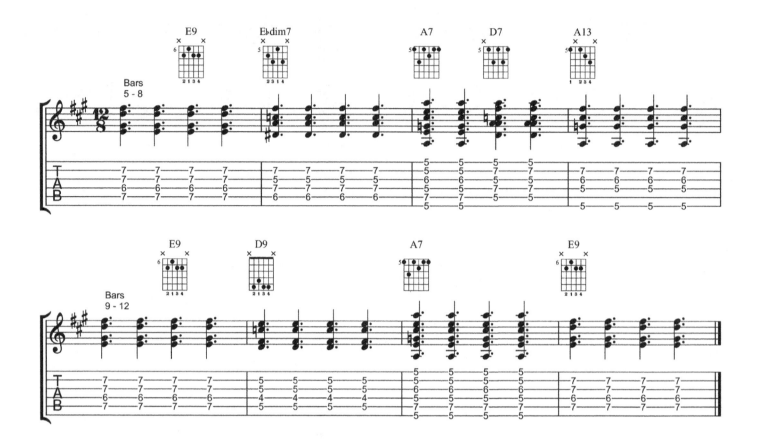

The musical tension in the 12-bar blues increases towards the end of the structure and the two E7 (V) chords are the ones most in need of resolution. As these chords are already tense, they are a great place to add *chromatic alterations* to further increase their pull back to the tonic.

A fantastic alteration we can add to the E7 chord to increase tension is a #9. You may already know E7#9 as the *Hendrix* chord that he used in songs such as Purple Haze and Foxy Lady. It is played like this on the guitar:

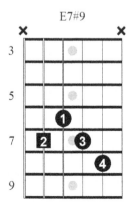

Try playing it as the final chord in the turnaround.

Example 6f:

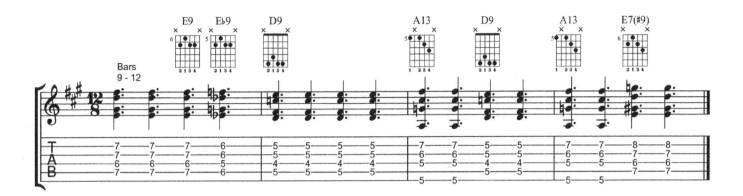

The next example is a little more 'jazzy' but I also like to use the 7#9 as a passing chord between D7 and F#7 in the following manner:

Example 6g:

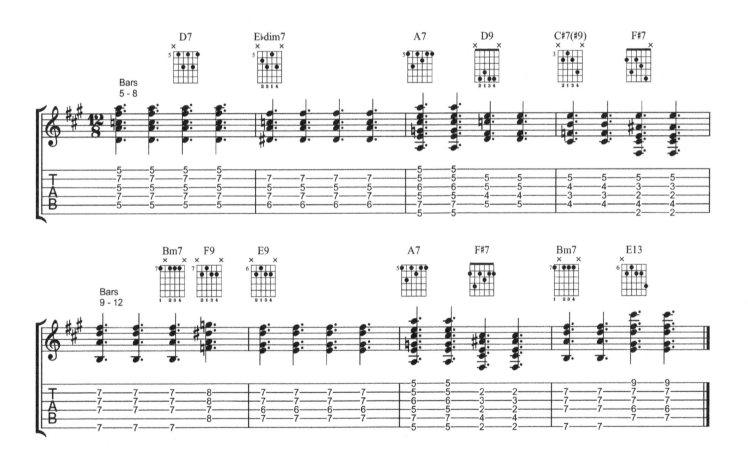

The examples in this section just scratch the surface of some more advanced jazz chord ideas but they represent some of the most common substitutions used in the 12-bar blues progression.

Chapter Seven – Rhythmic Placement with Triplet Blues

While the previous chapters have looked at harmonic ideas for the blues structure, we'll now look more closely at rhythm placement and concepts that you can apply to all your playing.

Triplet Blues

You'll remember that we count "1 2 3 1 2 3 1 2 3 1 2 3" through each bar in a triplet-style 12-bar blues. Everything is grouped in threes and this is the reason that we call this style a *triplet* feel. If you're not already comfortable with this idea, listen to Backing Track 4 and count the triplet feel out loud as described above.

As strange as it may seem at first, each of the three divisions of the beat is considered to be an 1/8th note.

There are three 1/8th notes or *quavers* per beat. Three 1/8th notes in a single beat doesn't make mathematical sense in the real world but it is an extremely important concept to understand in The Blues.

In example 7a, the top row of notes shows the main beat or pulse of the music, and the bottom row shows how the three 1/8th notes fit into each beat.

Example 7a:

Four beats x **three 1/8th notes** per beat = **twelve 1/8th notes per bar**.

This is what the *time signature* of 12/8 means: Twelve 1/8th notes per bar.

That's enough maths! Let's look at placing chords on some of these rhythmic subdivisions.

One simple way to play blues rhythm guitar that we have already covered is to strum only on each beat of the bar.

Example 7b:

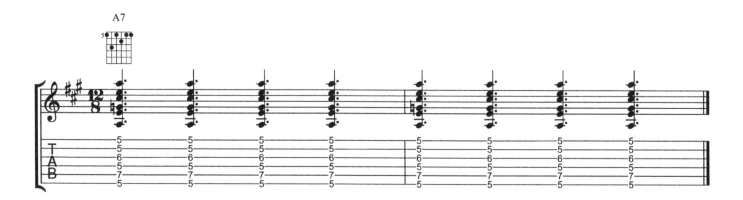

We can add more interest by playing on each of the triplet subdivisions. Use down-strokes to strum the following pattern.

Example 7c:

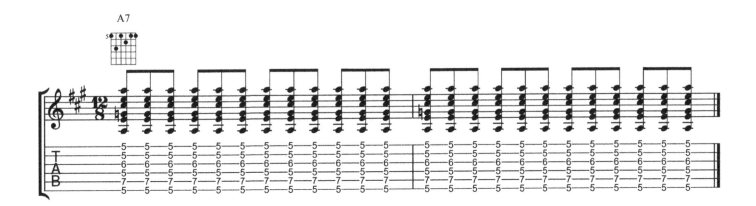

This adds more movement but it's very busy. Try playing on only the first and third triplet in each beat.

Example 7d:

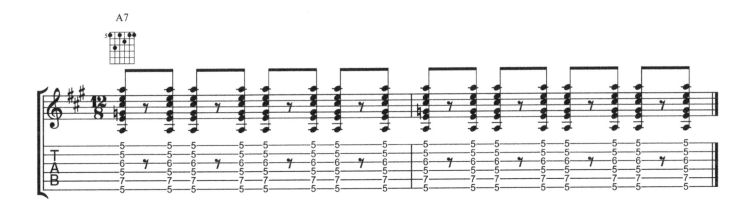

Listen to the audio example if you're not sure how to play this idea.

Personally, I feel that in most band situations it's best to leave a lot of space in the rhythm guitar part. By playing sparsely, especially at the beginning of a tune, it gives the song room to grow. Here are some patterns that use the triplet rhythms, but also leave large gaps that can be filled by other instruments.

Example 7e:

Example 7f

Example 7g:

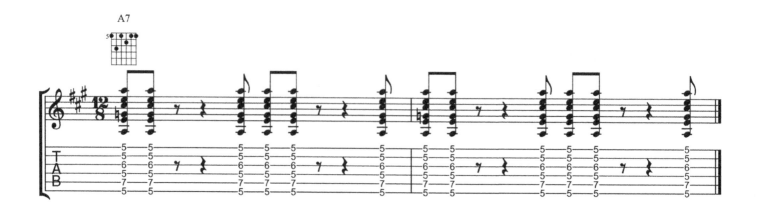

Example 7h:

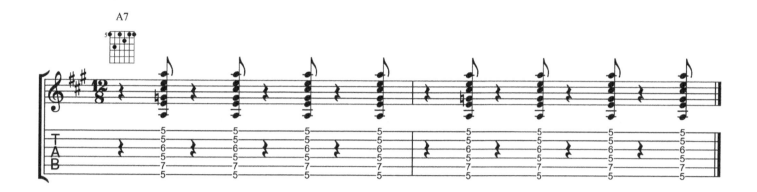

It's easy to add percussive *scratches* to the picking hand pattern. Hold the chord but release the pressure on the strings with your fretting hand while your strumming hand pattern plays a tight triplet feel. Scratched notes are notated with an 'x'.

Example 7i:

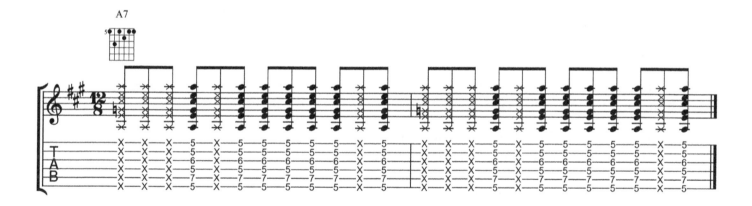

Even though I have notated the full chord, I will normally only play the highest four strings on the guitar to stay out of the way of the bass player. Try examples 7d to 7i again but this time play only the top four strings and add muted strums in some of the spaces.

Take some of these patterns through a whole 12-bar chorus. Try making your own rhythm patterns by missing out different combinations of triplets. These patterns can be as sparse or as dense as you like.

1/16th Note Subdivisions of the Beat

Each of the three 1/8th notes in the beat can be divided and split into two 1/16th notes to make a total of six subdivisions for each main pulse.

Example 7j:

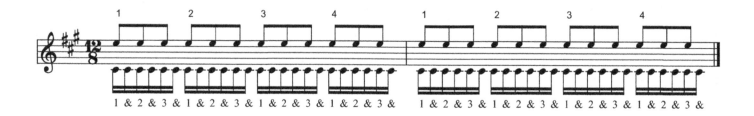

The top line in this example shows the triplet divisions and the bottom line shows how each triplet can be evenly divided into two subdivisions.

Count this out loud by saying "**1**and2and3and**1**and2and3and", etc.

Strum this rhythm with muted strings in the following way:

Down_updownupdownup_ **Down**_updownupdownup_.

Accent the first down stroke of each beat and ensure you can play in time with the audio from example 7j.

Blues rhythms based on 1/16th note subdivisions create many interesting strumming patterns but it's important not to overpower the rest of the band so use discretion and space in your playing.

To keep me in time and help with my dynamics I play quiet, muted strums on _every_ 1/16th note and accentuate the chords I wish to play with an unmuted chord.

To get the feel for this, play through the following example and mute every single stum.

Example 7k:

Next try to quietly play _all_ the subdivisions with an A7 chord without overpowering the drums and bass. Relax your wrist and remember that you don't have to play every string. Accent each main pulse (down beat) in the bar.

Example 7l:

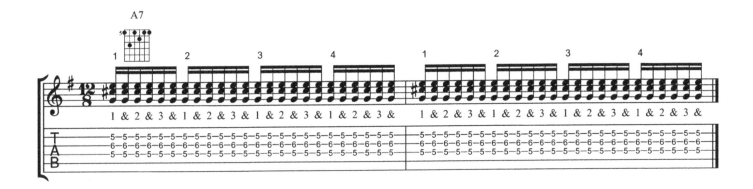

Now we will combine some 1/8th note and 1/16th note ideas. Try taking these patterns throughout the whole 12-bar progression.

Example 7m:

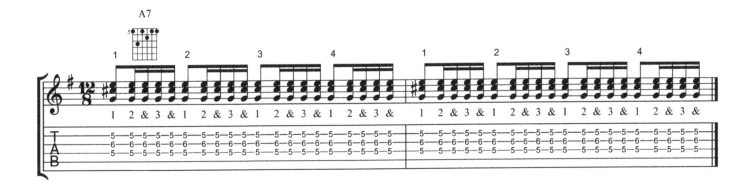

Example 7n:

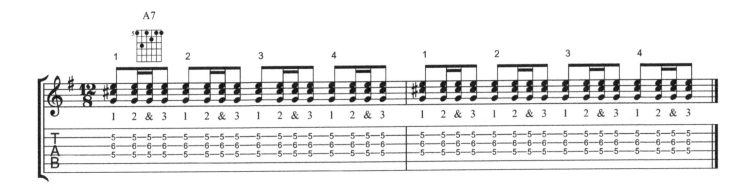

Now combine the percussive scratches with chord stabs. In the following examples, muted notes are notated with an *x*.

The first idea is quite challenging as it's very syncopated. Start slowly and gradually build up the speed when you get into the feel of the rhythm. Remember; keep your scratches light and accentuate the chord stabs.

Example 7o:

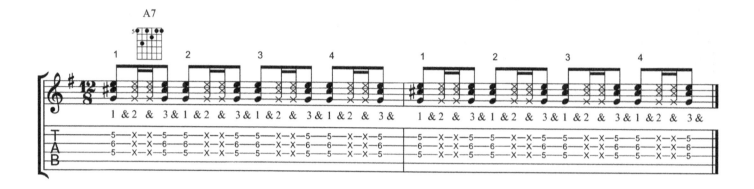

Example 7p:

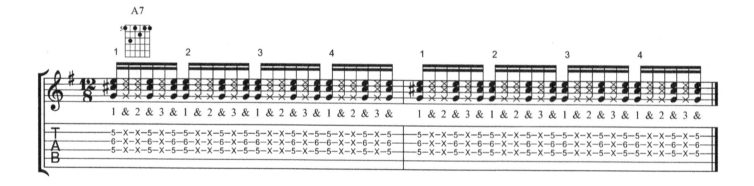

Example 7q:

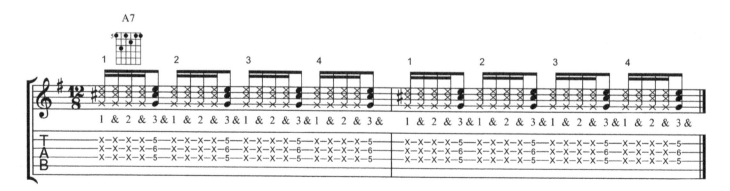

Often, we don't want to play a note *or* a scratch on a beat because sometimes the music requires silence. You can *mime* 1/16th notes in the same way you played the 1/16th note scratches. Move your strumming hand up and down in time, simply do not connect with the guitar strings. This is a great way to stay in time and develop control and placement with your strums.

Example 7r contains a 1/16th note rest in beat one. Keep your strumming hand moving throughout, but don't connect with the strings on the rests.

Example 7r:

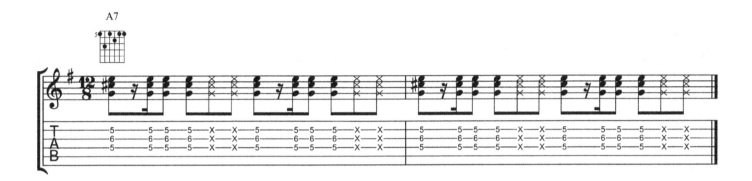

We can still use rhythmic ideas like sliding chords from a semitone below. These create a 'sub-rhythm' against the main groove of the rhythm part.

Example 7s:

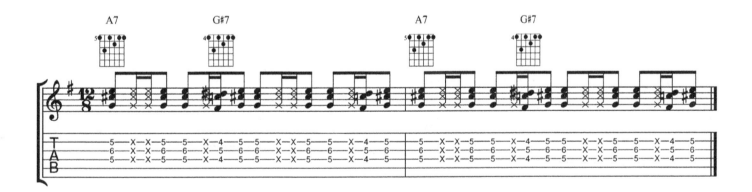

Use the strumming patterns in this chapter to play through full 12-blues progressions. Don't be afraid to alter or combine them, and don't forget that a rhythm pattern can be more than one bar long.

The best thing to do is to listen to your favourite recordings and copy the style the rhythm players you like.

Chapter Eight – Rhythmic Placement with Straight Blues

In a *straight* time feel, each beat in the bar is split into *even* subdivisions. Whereas a triplet feel is split into rhythmic groupings of three, a straight feel is split into rhythmic groupings of two and four.

In example 8a the top line of music shows the main 1/4 note (crotchet) beat of the bar and the bottom line shows how each beat is divided into two subdivisions.

Example 8a:

Look at the 4/4 time signature. If a time signature has the number 4 at the bottom then the convention is to group the subdivisions into even rhythmic divisions.

Begin by strumming on just the first beat of each bar. Although this is a similar exercise to example 7b you will find that this rhythm feels quite different when played with a straight drum groove. Remember, you don't have to play the full chord, often just the top four strings will do.

Example 8b:

We can add more movement by playing on each 1/8th note (quaver) subdivision.

Example 8c:

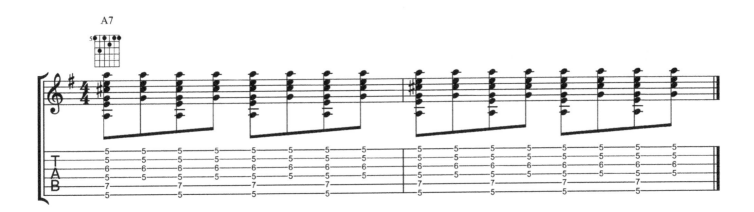

Playing on each 1/8th note can be a little too rhythmically dense, so here are some patterns that use 1/8th notes but don't include a strum on every subdivision of the beat. Take these rhythm figures through the full 12-bar blues chord sequence and play along with Backing Track 1: Straight Blues in A.

Example 8d:

Example 8e:

Example 8f:

Example 8g:

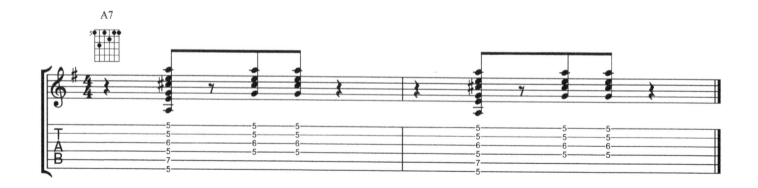

Once again, we can use scratches to add percussive rhythms to the chords and to help us stay in time. In the following examples, I split the chord so that I play the bass strings and the high strings separately.

Example 8h:

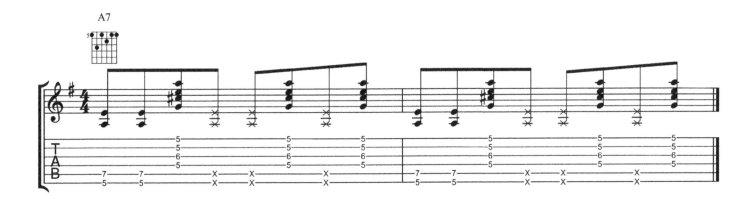

Example 8i:

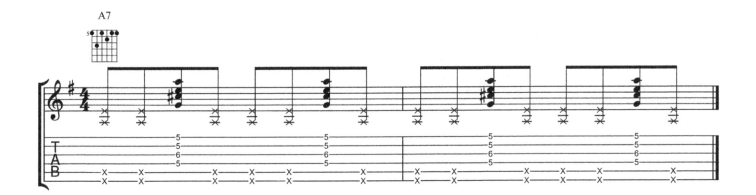

Example 8j:

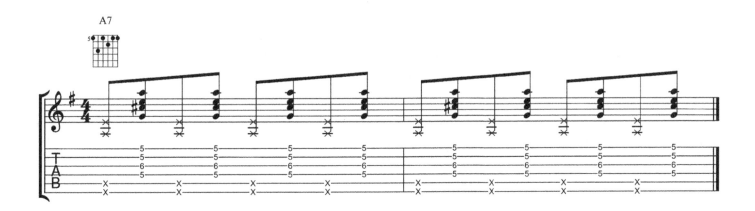

1/16th Note Subdivisions of the Beat

As with triplets, each 1/8th note can be split further into 1/16th notes.

To get a feel for this rhythm count "1 e and a 2 e and a 3 e and a 4 e and a" out loud along with Backing Track 1.

Try strumming this rhythm with muted strings. Throughout the whole bar your strumming should be

Downupdownup**down**updownup

Example 8k:

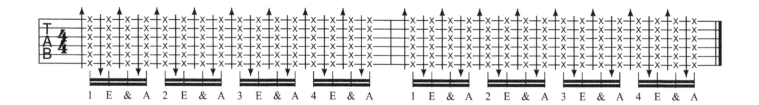

Now let's study some strumming patterns that use combinations of 1/16th notes and 1/8th notes. Play these rhythms throughout the whole 12-bar progression.

Example 8l:

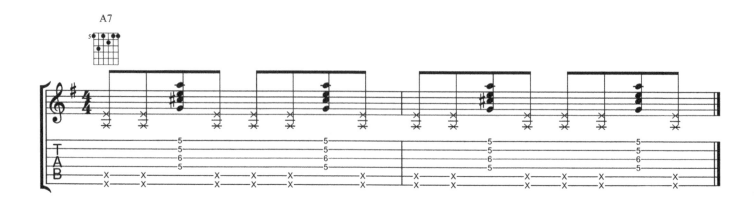

Example 8m:

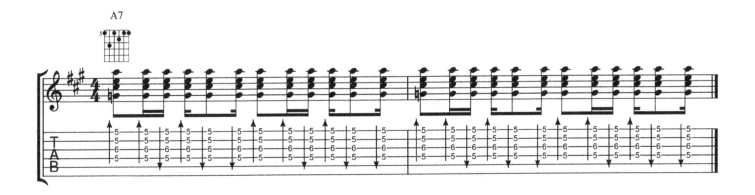

Example 8n:

Example 8o:

Example 8p is a bit trickier than the earlier examples. Listen carefully to the audio and keep your strumming hand moving in 1/16th notes, whether you are connecting with the strings or not.

Example 8p:

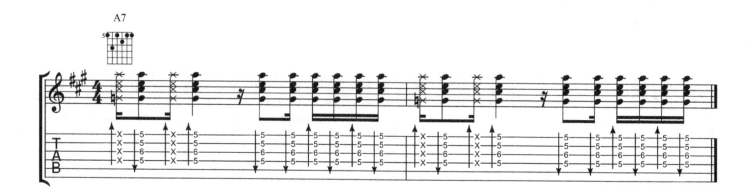

1/16th Note Shuffle Grooves

The 1/16th note divisions of each beat do not have to be evenly spaced.

If the first of each group of two 1/16th notes is longer and the second shorter, the rhythm is said to be a *shuffle*. Shuffle rhythms can look identical on paper to straight 1/16ths, but there is normally a performance direction at the start of the music such as the word *shuffle* above the first bar.

Listen to example 8q and compare it to example 8k. Whereas example 8k is completely straight, example 8q has a definite bounce to it.

Example 8q:

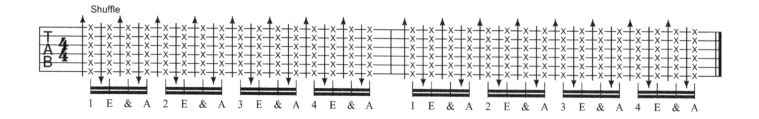

The following rhythm is the same as in exercise 80, however this time the rhythm is played with a shuffle feel.

Example 8r:

Shuffle

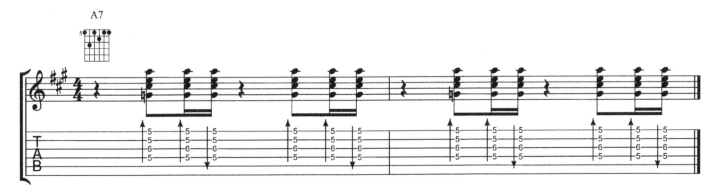

Chapter Nine – Melodic Fills between Chords

Rhythm guitar playing isn't just about playing chords; we can *decorate* the chords we play with single-note phrases to provide movement and countermelody to the singer or soloist.

The art is not to over-play, and to ensure our playing is appropriate to the music. There should always be space for the main melody of the song to shine through. In fact, overplaying and cluttering the melody is one of the easiest ways to get kicked out of a band!

The idea is to play in the spaces left by the singer, so don't try to fill every possible gap, and roll your volume down so as not to overpower everyone else on stage.

Fills on the I Chord

The following rhythm fills work well on a static I chord. This is the A7 chord in a blues in A. Play them in other keys too.

Example 9a:

Example 9b:

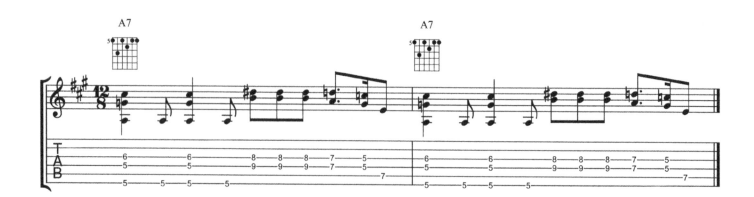

Example 9c:

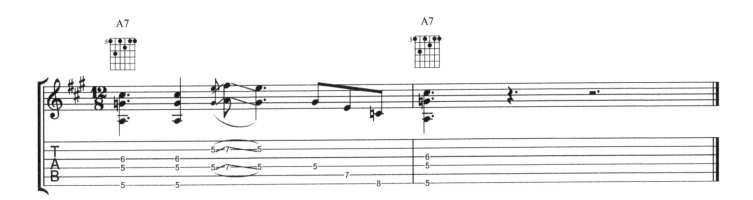

Fills on the IV Chord

These licks target important notes of the IV (D7) chord, however you can shift them all up by one tone so they work on the V (E7) chord.

Example 9d:

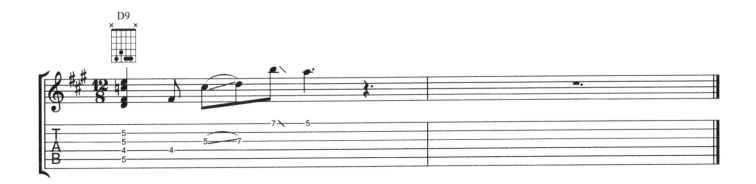

Example 9e:

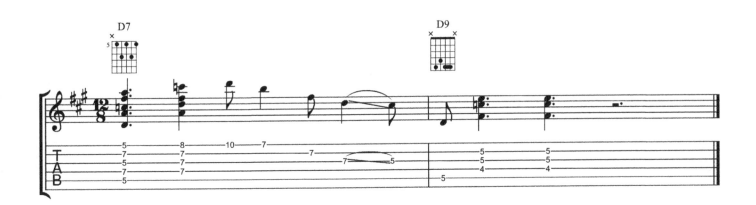

Example 9f:

Fills on the V Chord

Again, you can shift these V-chord (E7) lines *down* one tone and they work well as D7 licks.

Example 9g:

Example 9h:

Example 9i:

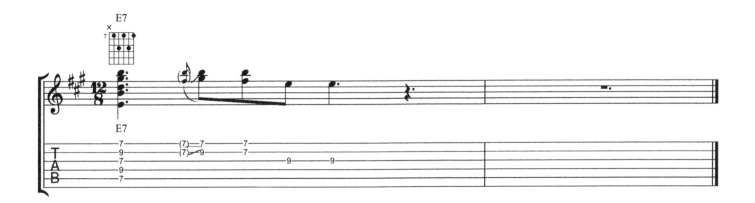

Fills Moving from Chord I to IV

The following ideas are used to target notes while moving from the I chord (A7) to the IV chord (D7).

Example 9j:

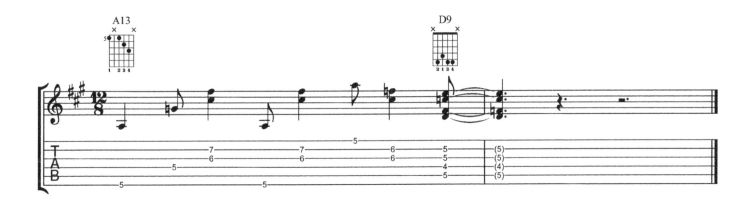

Example 9k:

Example 9l:

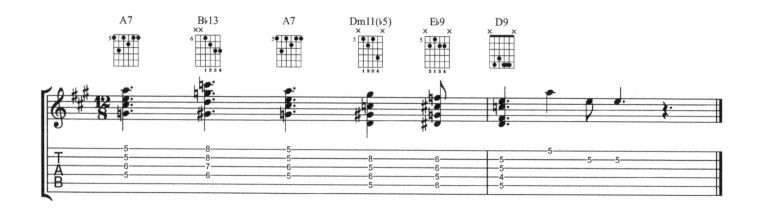

Fills Moving from Chord IV to I

These licks fill in the gaps when moving from IV (D7) back to I (A7).

Example 9m:

Example 9n:

Fills Moving from Chord V to IV

The following examples add melodic interest when moving from (V) E7 to (IV) D7.

Example 9o:

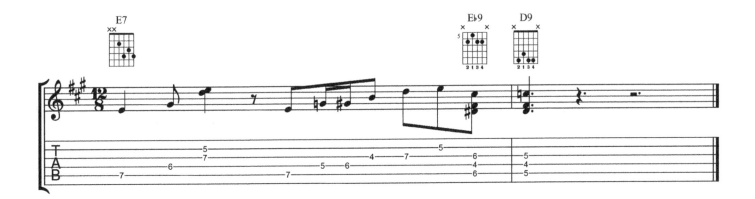

Example 9p:

Fills Moving from Chord I to V

These fills create strong melodic voice leading when moving from chord I (A7) to the all-important V (E7) chord.

Example 9q:

Example 9r:

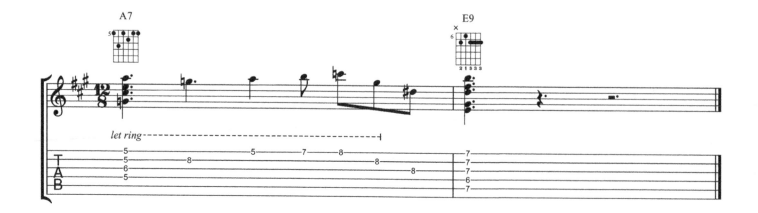

Example 9s:

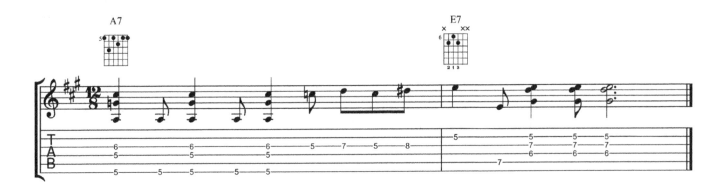

The occasional melodic line leading from one chord to another or over a prolonged period on a static chord will give great contrast to a repetitive rhythm guitar part. Notice how most of the lines only occur towards the end of the bar; the crucial concept is to leave space for your singer or soloist.

Chapter Ten – Intros and Outros

Being able to begin and end a tune cleanly saves a lot of embarrassment on stage and helps to reinforce a memorable performance. Too many times I have seen under-rehearsed bands frantically looking at each other trying to find someone to take control and actually lead the tune they are playing to a satisfying conclusion. With some stock outros (and intros) you'll always be able to find a way to end a song cleanly.

Intros to many songs are often based on the final few chords or turnaround section of the song. There is a bit of a crossover in the following examples between what is considered 'lead' guitar and what is considered rhythm guitar playing but that is nothing to worry about.

Intros are extremely useful because they can always function as an outro too. It just depends on which chord you end on. For example, look at this intro in the key of A Major.

This idea is based around a descending Dominant 7th chord and ends with an E7 chord approached from a semitone above. By ending on the E7 (Dominant) chord we create the feeling that the music wants to continue by resolving back to A7.

Example 10a:

Now look at example 10b. This line begins in the same way but instead of ending on E7 as before, the line finishes on the A7 once again approached by step from above. This resolution has a certain degree of finality about it and it would be difficult to keep the music moving forward after this point.

Example 10b:

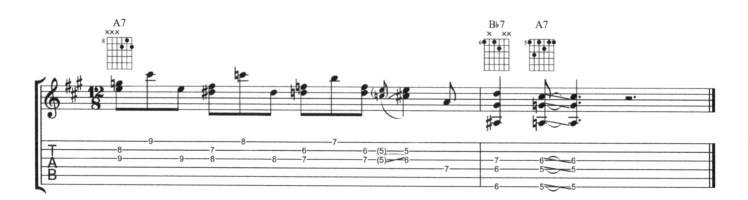

As you can hear, this is the musical equivalent of a period or full stop.

Alter all the following lines to end on A7 if you want use them as an outro instead of an intro.

The next example contains an A note *drone* as the bass line descends. The E7 is approached by a semitone from above but this time in a much lower voicing.

Example 10c:

If you end the lick with a Bb7 to A7 movement it will serve as a great final outro.

The next idea demonstrates a musical device called *contrary motion*. This is where two parts move in opposite melodic directions. Notice that the dominant chord is now approached from a semitone below.

Example 10d:

The next intro lick moves through ascending chords up to the Dominant chord E7.

Look out for a chord sequence you have seen before: The D Major becomes an E Dim7 chord before moving to the E7. This creates the chromatic bass line C#, D, Eb, E which is an extremely strong harmonic movement.

Example 10e:

Instead of an approach chord into the E7 there is a short A Mixolydian lick that leads smoothly into the change.

Next, melodic movement is created at the top of the chord by careful use of chord voicings. I would normally pick a line like this with the fingers of my picking hand.

On beats 3 and 4 there is a movement from chord IV Major (D) to chord iv Minor (Dm). This rich-sounding change is an ear-catching addition to the phrase. Try to accentuate the string which contains the melody note.

Example 10f:

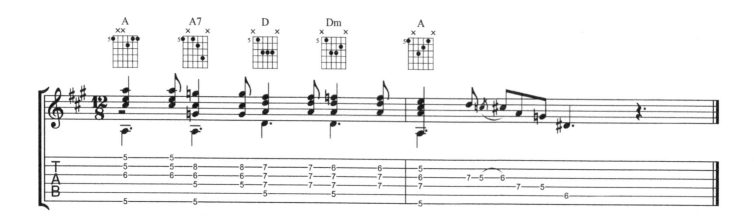

While there is no obvious E7 chord in example 10f, the lick at the end *targets* the note G# with an important *guide tone* of the chord. Targeting the G# makes the listener believe they have heard the dominant chord in its entirety, and that the song is ready to begin.

To change this intro lick into an outro lick I could simply approach an A7 by step at the end of the l...

Example 10g:

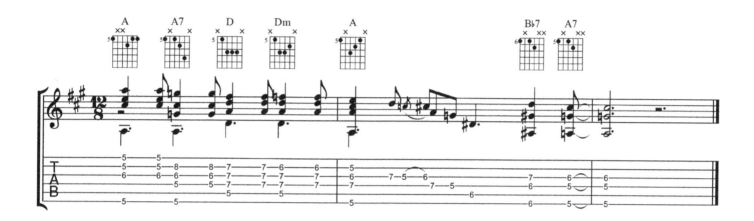

If in doubt it's hard to go wrong with this Jimi Hendrix-style ending. This example uses ascending power chords to move up to the dominant chord but ends with some big '9' chords for a rockier ending.

Example 10h:

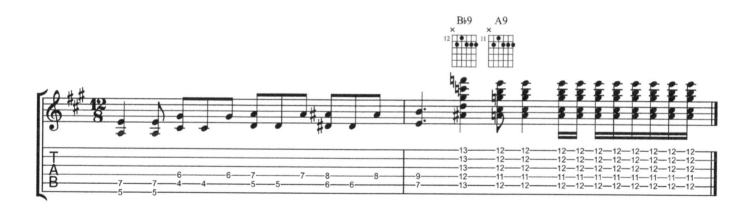

Convert this lick to an intro line by changing the Bb9 and Ab9 to an F9 and E9.

Clean intros and endings are an important part of a tight band performance. Always rehearse exactly what you'll play for each song before you get on stage.

There's nothing worse than a sloppy ending to a song and the audience will probably remember that, rather than your ground-breaking guitar solo. It's essential to get the basic building-blocks of the song right.

Chapter Eleven – Shell Voicings

we'll all experience in our musical career is the 'busy blues jam-night'. We could find ourselves
two other guitarists, a keyboard player, a bass guitar, three singers and a flugel horn. It can be
gh to know what and indeed *when* to play a chord.

The rhythm section can be so crowded that it is almost impossible to play anything that enhances the music and makes the audience's experience better. If it is really that busy on stage, my best piece of advice is to not play anything at all. Playing muted, rhythmic scratches on deadened strings can work, but often it's best to leave some space. This is a legitimate musical decision and one that is often for the greater good.

You may find yourself in a band where things are quite busy but (hopefully) a little less dense. In these circumstances, I often find myself playing sparsely and using *shell voicings*, or *drop two* chords.

Shell voicings contain only the root, 3rd and b7 of a chord. They do not contain the 5th or any extensions.

The 3rd and 7th are the two notes that define the chord quality, be it Major, Minor or Dominant. No other notes are needed, not even the root. In fact, I often avoid playing the root altogether if I'm playing with a bass player.

In this section, you'll learn to play different shell voicing shapes for the chords in the 12-bar blues. They are fantastic to use rhythmically when we don't have much space in the band to play bigger chords. Shell voicings also tend to automatically create smooth voice leading between chord changes.

Here are some shell voicings for an A7 chord.

Example 11a:

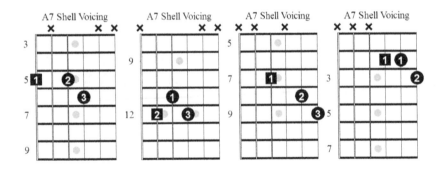

These shapes are movable so they can be treated like barre chords. For example, you could play through the chords in a blues by just using the movable shape on the 6th string.

Example 11b:

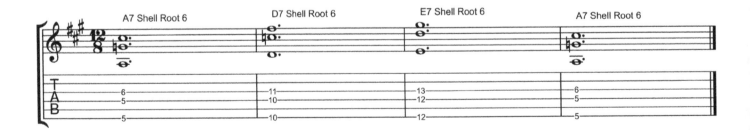

The jumps in the example above are a little large, so let's play these chords in one position on the neck.

Example 11c:

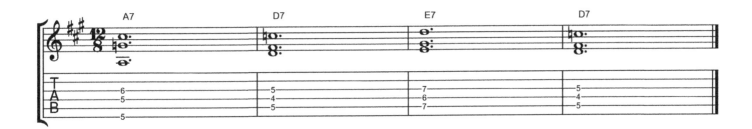

Play these chord shapes in a full blues progression and remember, all the rhythmic and approach ideas are still available. Here's just one way to navigate the 12-bar blues with shell voicings.

Example 11d:

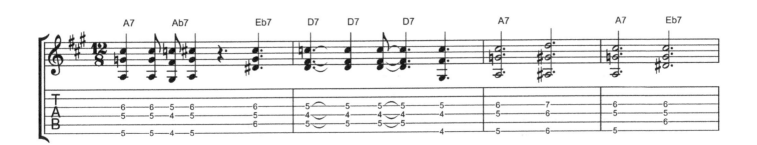

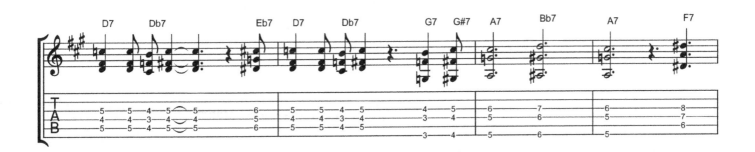

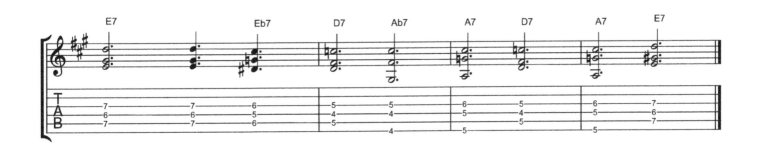

The previous example is deliberately simple. It provides just enough movement to keep things interesting as a self-contained study although you may wish to play even less in a busy band situation.

We haven't yet explored shell voicings on higher string groups. Here's how to play the chords on the top three and four strings.

Example 11e:

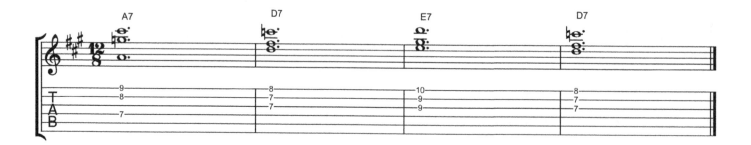

Here are the shell voicings for Bm7.

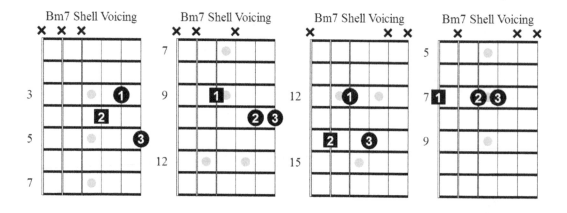

You now have all the voicings you need to play an extended blues. The next example teaches you to navigate the chords in a 12-bar blues with a 1 6 2 5 turnaround. Once the chord voicings are memorised, add in your own rhythms and approach chords to make the music personal.

Remember, the whole idea behind this approach is to keep things simple and to leave room for others to play.

Example 11f:

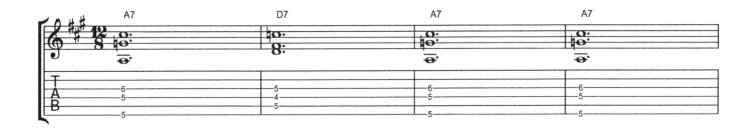

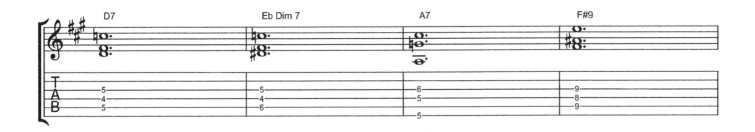

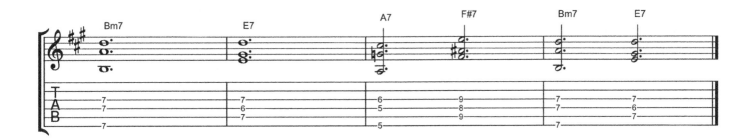

Next, try finding as many ways as you can through the changes using shell voicings on different string groups. Begin with the root of the first chord on either the 6th, 5th, 4th or 3rd string, and then try to find the closest possible voicing of the next chord to move to.

You can play just the 3rds and 7ths of each chord without including the bass notes.

This idea is useful because it teaches you to see the most important notes of the chord as closely linked shapes.

For example, here are the last four bars of the previous example played with just the 3rds and b7s:

Example 11g:

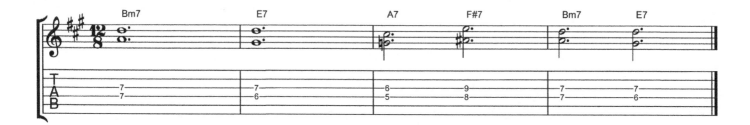

When I teach my students these movements on the guitar, it often comes as a surprise to them to see just how closely these chords are all related. These guide tones can also be used as soloing ideas to melodically outline each chord.

Spend some serious practice time working out how to play closely-voiced guide tone lines on each two-string grouping. For example, try to play through the 12-bar blues using only 3rds and 7ths on the first and second strings. Then play them on the second and third strings, the third and fourth strings, and finally fourth and fifth strings.

Chapter Twelve – Drop 2 Voicings

We have now used shell voicings to keep out of the way of a busy rhythm section and played them in low-register voicings to not crowd the range where singers and soloists play.

Drop 2 chords are another way to stay clear of dense harmony parts, but these are normally played in a *higher* register where the tone of the guitar isn't as heavy. Drop 2 chords are useful at higher tempos where we might play more percussive chord stabs rather than letting chords ring out.

Drop 2 voicings are simply an arranging technique where the second highest note in a chord is dropped by an octave. For example, here is the chord of A7 as a stacked *closed position* voicing:

When we drop the second highest note down an octave, the chord becomes a drop 2 voicing:

Once again, this isn't a theory book, for more information you may wish to check out my book **Drop 2 Chord Voicings for Jazz and Modern Guitar.**

It is common for drop 2 chords to be played on the top four strings, but it is a worthwhile pursuit to explore them on the middle four strings too.

Any four-note drop 2 chord can be played in any of four inversions. This gives four different ways to play each chord.

These are the four drop 2 voicings of an A7 chord arranged from the lowest position on the neck to the highest. The square dot in each chord is the root and it is only the bass note in one of the voicings.

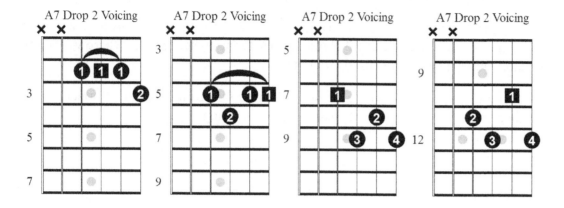

Play through all four voicings in the following way:

Example 12a:

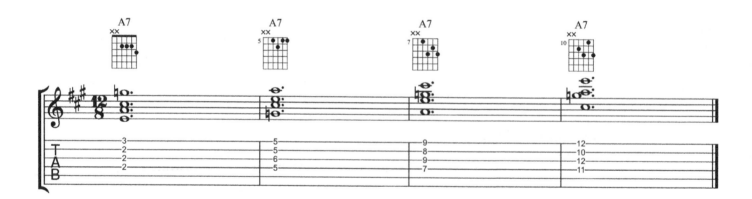

Next, link together the chords in the 12-bar blues using the closest available shape for each chord. Beginning on each voicing of A7 in turn we quickly discover four closely related ways to play the I, IV, V progression with minimum movement.

Example 12b:

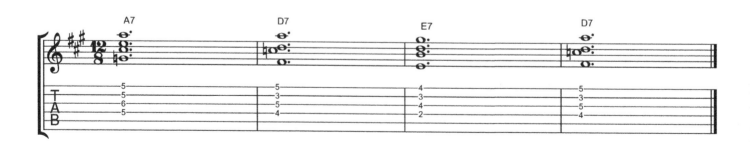

Example 12c:

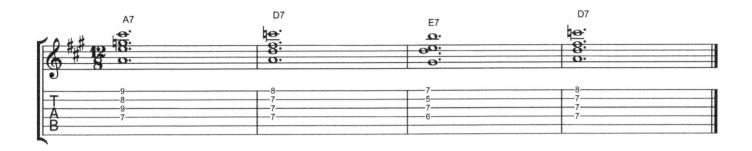

Example 12d:

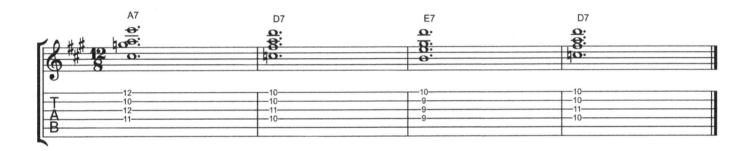

Example 12e:

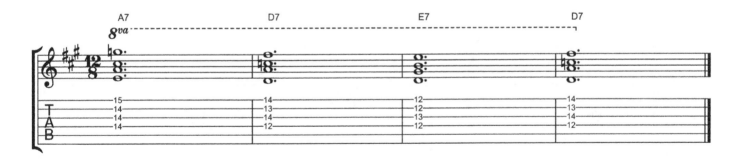

Knowing how to move between chords I, IV and V in four positions is essential, because you now have the whole neck covered. It's always possible to move to a nearby voicing when the chords change and makes for a very intelligent, smooth-sounding guitar part.

You can always use more than one chord per bar to create a melody line with the top note of each voicing.

Notice how I keep the melody flowing by approaching all the chords with stepwise chord slides from above or below to help. These ideas are totally limitless; a good grasp of drop 2 chords all over the neck is very useful for creating an interesting and *melodic* rhythm part without an overly dense chord sound.

Example 12f:

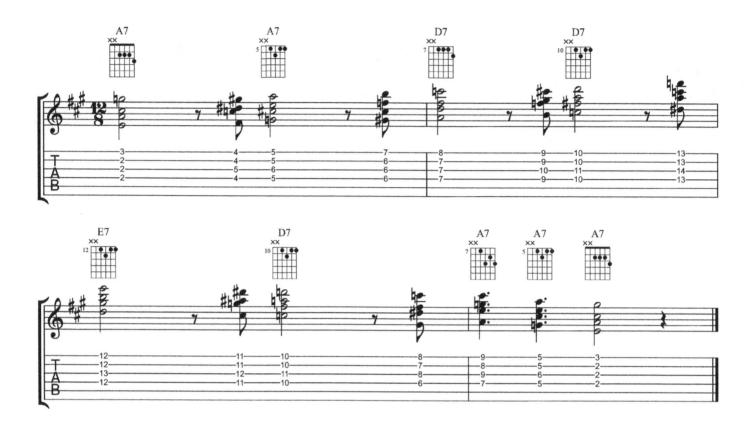

Add in the drop 2 voicings for the Bm7 chord and use these in the same way:

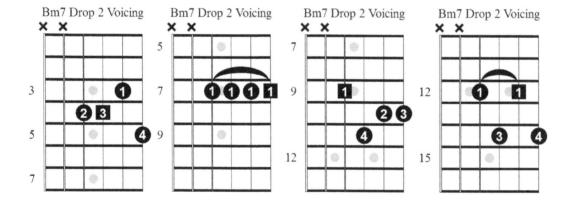

Here is one way to play the I VI II V turnaround in the key of A:

Example 12g:

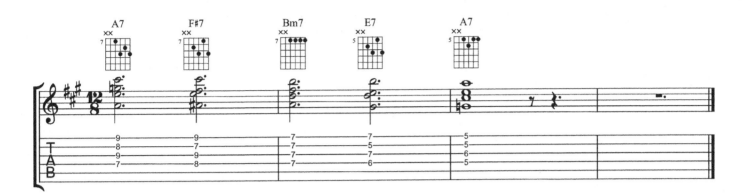

As with the earlier examples, try to find as many ways to play through this chord progression. Take it in turns to start from a different voicing of the A7 chord.

Here are some sample rhythm patterns you could use with drop 2 voicings.

Example 12h:

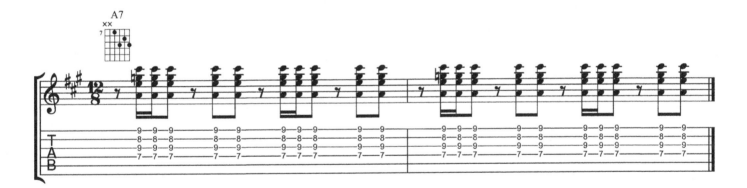

Example 12i:

Example 12j:

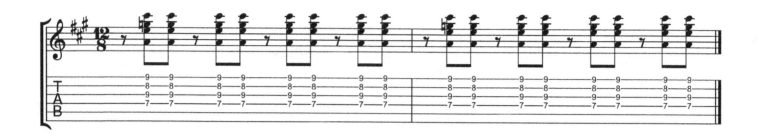

Of course, the rhythm pattern you play will depend on the groove of the song, so use your ears and lock in with the band.

Chapter Thirteen - The Minor Blues

Until now we have been mainly examining the 12-bar blues played with Dominant 7 chords. These are probably the most common type of blues chords but there is one more important blues style you should know.

The whole 12-bar progression can be based around minor chords to create a dark, sombre mood. It is acceptable to play *every* chord in this progression as a minor chord, however a Dominant V chord (E7) is often used to add tension before resolving to the tonic chord (A7).

Here is the structure for a basic Minor blues.

Example 13a:

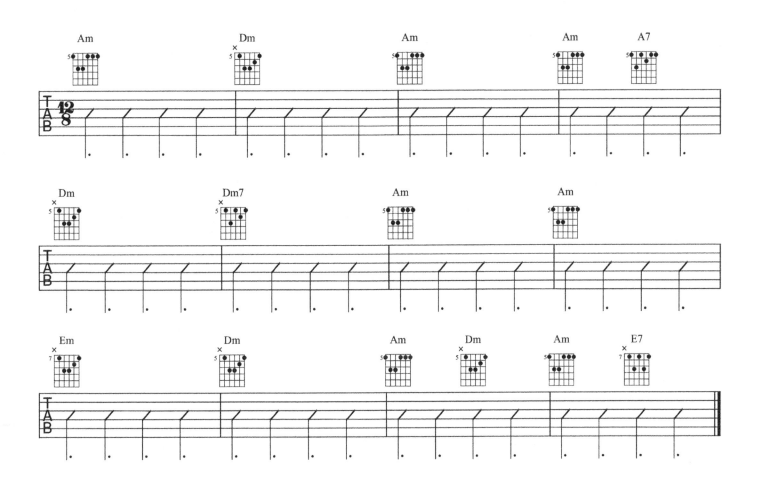

Notice how the change to A7 in bar four helps create a smooth transition into the Dm.

In bar six I use a Dm7 chord for a bit of colour, and in bar 12 I use an E7, not an Em to build the tension at the end of the turnaround.

Here's the new vocabulary you need to play the previous progression.

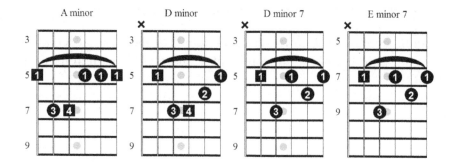

As with the dominant 7 blues there are many techniques we can use to add interest and movement to the minor blues progression.

Play through the following progression and look out for examples of

1) Substitutions

2) Approaching chords by step

3) Altered chords

4) Changing from minor to dominant chords in the same bar

Example 13b:

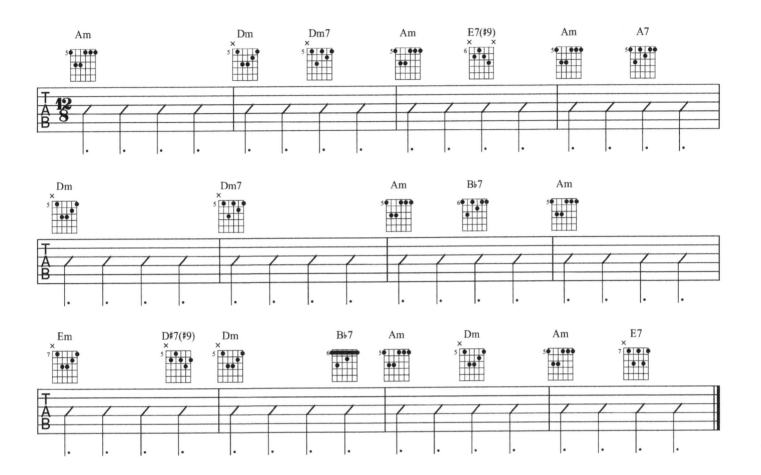

Listen to players such as Gary Moore and B.B. King as they used many variations of the Minor blues in their music.

The 8-bar Blues

The 12-bar blues is not the only blues structure. The 8-bar blues is used in many songs and is an important form to know. There are many variations but the basic structure is normally something like this.

Example 14a:

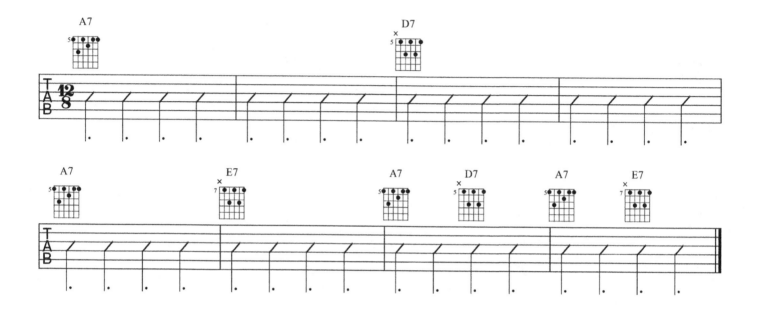

Here's another common variant:

Example 14b:

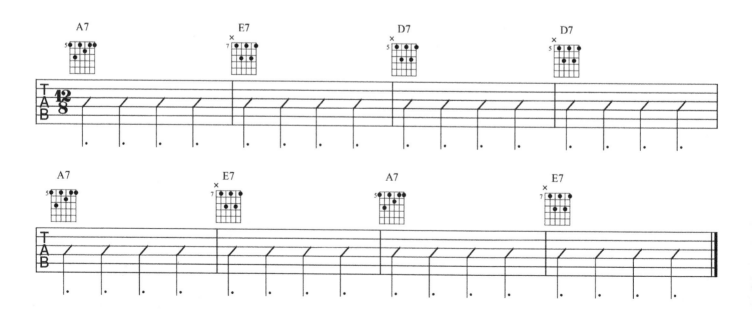

It is not uncommon to move from a Major IV chord (D Major or D7) to a Minor iv chord (D Minor or Dm7) in bar four.

Example 14c:

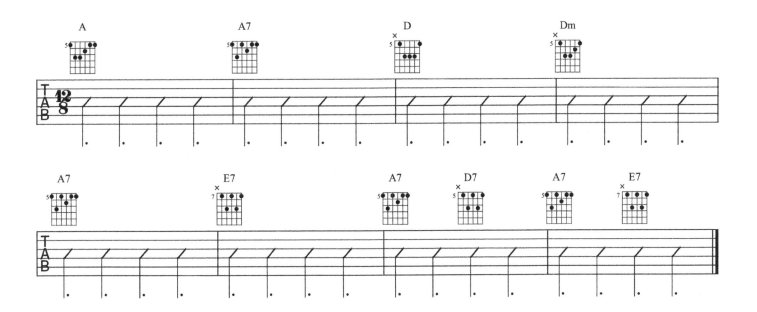

Here's chord vocabulary you need to play the previous example. Try swapping the D Minor for a D Minor 7.

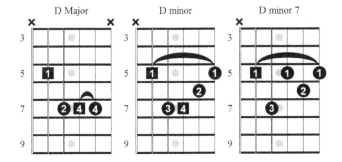

Just as we altered the chords and structure of the 12-bar blues, we can take a similar approach to playing the 8-bar form.

We can add an Eb Dim7 chord in bar four and a I VI II V turnaround in bars five and six. This time however, the VI chord (F#) is played as a minor chord instead of a dominant 7.

Example 14d:

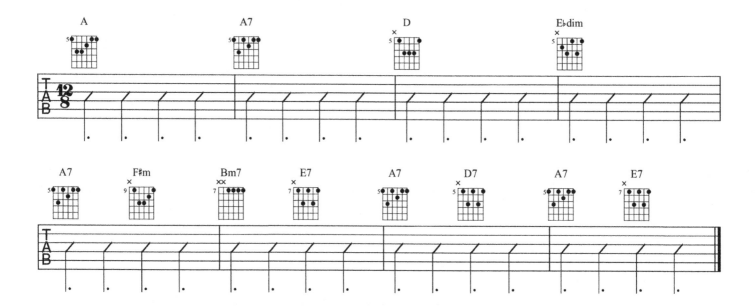

Of course, we can add in any of the harmonic ideas from the 12-bar blues too. Here is one way to add the bVI into bar six, and I've also spiced up the 7 chords with a few 9ths, 13ths, and approach chords.

The rhythm is deliberately simple so you can concentrate on mastering the new 8-bar form. Feel free to spice it up a bit. You may wish to use drop 2 chords and/or shell voicings on this tune too. There are many possible ways to vary this chord progression so don't take the following example as set in stone.

Example 14e:

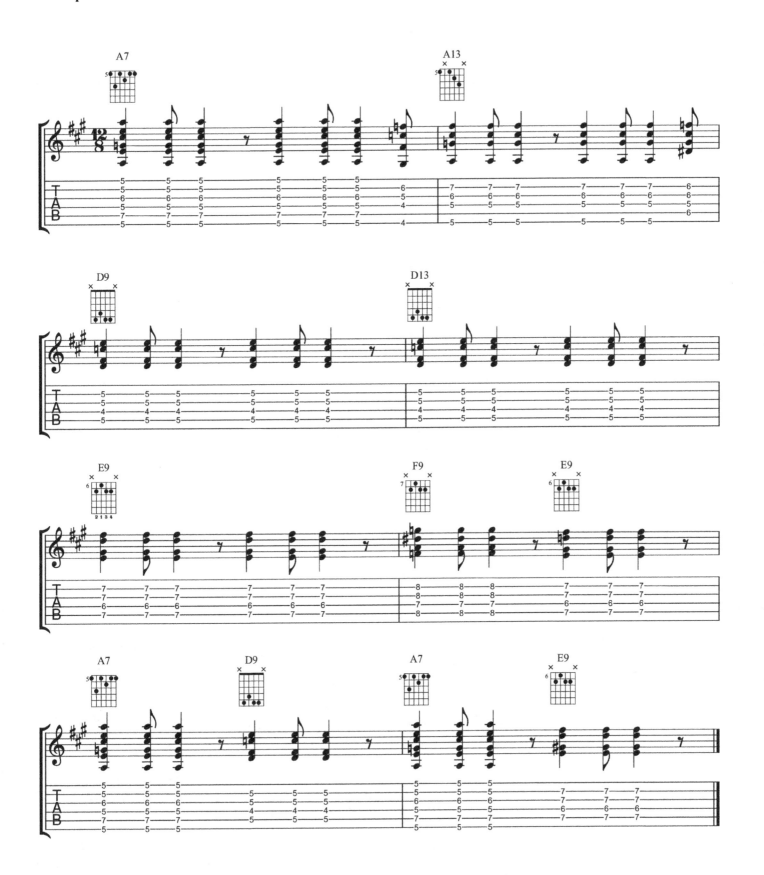

The 16-bar Blues

Another well-recognised blues form is the 16-bar blues. It is used in famous tunes such as Hoochie Coochie Man (Muddy Waters) and Oh Pretty Woman (A.C Williams).

Often the 16-bar blues is treated as a 12-bar with an extra 4-bar *tag* ending. A simple version of this is shown below.

Example 16f:

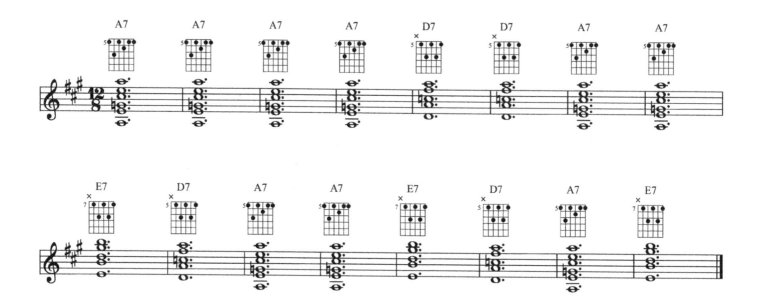

Other 16-bar forms may repeat the V to IV movement (Dominant to subdominant chords) in bars nine to fourteen.

Example 14g:

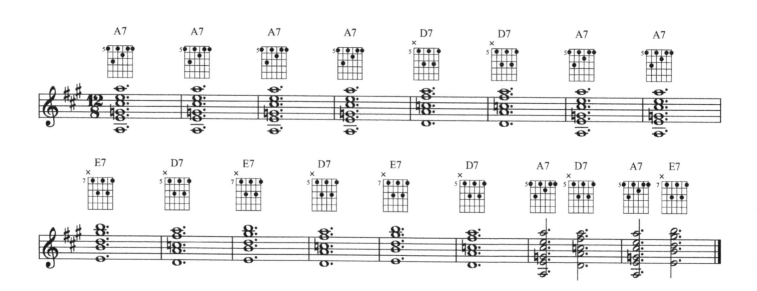

You will also find 16-bar blues sequences that stay on the I chord (A7) for eight bars. This is a great opportunity use of drop 2 chord voicings in different inversions and create a melody at the top of the chords, just like you did in example 12f.

Example 14h:

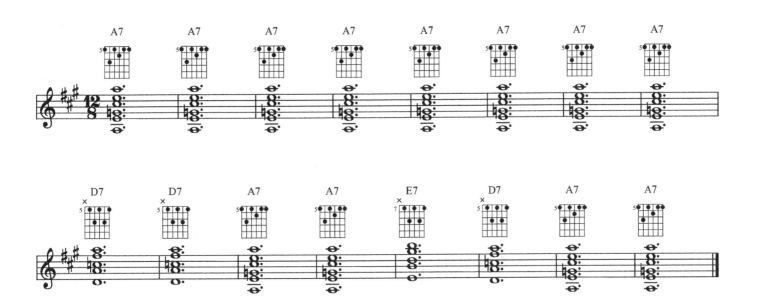

It's quite common to find this type of progression in pop or rock tunes as sometimes writers don't want a lot of harmonic movement at the start of the verse.

Chapter Fifteen – Conclusions

This book has been written to take you from the first principles of the basic 12-bar blues right through to some complex chord substitutions, rhythms and melodic fills. The emphasis has been on fitting in with the band, adding to the groove and considering what to play and what to leave out.

It is normally the case that less is more. The guitar is also a percussive instrument, so don't be afraid to fill in the gaps with rhythmic scratches, sparse chords and, if in doubt, silence. You don't have to play every chord if there is another instrument there to do it for you.

Each time you play, either in practice or in the band, record your sessions and notice what your guitar part is adding to the music. You may feel that you should play more *or* less, that you need to work more or less closely with the bass and drums, or maybe just provide the harmonic padding of playing one chord per bar.

It's OK to call a band meeting to decide exactly what and when each instrument is playing. Of course, there should always be room for spontaneity and improvisation in The Blues, but time spent in the rehearsal room building the track from the ground up can quickly revolutionise your band's sound.

In rehearsals, I normally like to begin with only the drummer playing. Next, I bring in the bass, and when they start locking together, that's when I bring in the harmonic instruments. There are no hard and fast rules but I like to get the keyboard player to play first so I can work my part around them.

Having both a guitar and keyboard in a band can be a challenge because both instruments take up so much sonic 'real estate'. Ask the keyboard player to play with just his right hand if things are getting too crowded in the guitar frequencies, or, if he is already playing higher voicings of the chords you can stick to shell voicings on the guitar.

If there are two guitarists in the band don't both play the same thing. Either sit out or arrange things so that you're using different approaches in different registers. For example, if one guitar is playing an open string riff, you may wish to play drop 2 chord pads or rhythmic staccato chops. You may want to take care of the melodic fills between chords or play the odd blues lick between the vocals, a la B.B. King. Don't overplay; save it for the solo.

If you're covering someone else's song, listen to as many different artist's recordings of it as possible. Discover what instrumentation they've used, and how they've interpreted the track in their own unique way. This process will guide you towards finding the identity you want as a musician.

I've given a list of essential listening below that should help you understand The Blues and allow you to discover your own sound. However, to give a list of definitive musicians is, quite frankly, impossible. I've tried to include specific artists and albums that you should know, but this list is by no means exhaustive so please don't send me hate mail if your favourite artist isn't here!

Don't forget, what might be considered rock music today definitely has its roots in blues. Check out bands like Led Zeppelin, Cream, Pink Floyd, The Who and AC/DC. Hear their blues influences and listen to what makes their music crossover into Rock.

For the sake of easy communication, most of the examples in this book have been written in the key of A. However, The Blues can be played in *any* key. Some of the more common keys are E, G, and C, but if there is a brass or woodwind instrument in the band you may be asked to play in Bb, Eb, Ab or Db. Any barre chord forms in this book are movable, but if a riff uses open strings you may need to be creative about using those ideas. At a pinch, you can always grab a capo.

Many blues (and indeed rock) tunes are in the key of Eb and are played with open string riffs on the guitar. This is achieved by tuning the guitar down a half step to become Eb, Ab, Db, Gb, Bb and Eb from low to high. There are a few reasons for this: Firstly, the male vocal range can be quite comfortable in that tuning but the main reason is that a Fender Stratocaster in Eb tuning with thick strings (try 11s or 13s!) and a cranked-up amp sings beautifully. Normally I keep a spare guitar tuned to Eb if I need to transcribe a solo or do a short-notice gig. Stevie Ray Vaughan and Jimi Hendrix, among many others are famous for tuning down to Eb.

Guitar tone is another important consideration. I could fill another book just talking about tone, but suffice to say that for blues rhythm guitar, depending on context, I use a clean-ish sound that starts to break up slightly when I strum a bit harder.

Try using your volume control as an extra tone control. Not enough guitarists are aware of the fun you can have with a cranked-up amp controlled by clever use of your volume knob and the many different textures that it creates.

The best piece of advice I can give anyone is to listen as much as you can to the style you wish to play. Transcribe rhythm guitar parts, even if it's just the guitarist's rhythm you focus on. Playing a different chord voicing is insignificant when compared to the benefit you get by locking into your favourite player's groove.

Have fun and good luck.

Joseph

Recommended Listening

Albert Collins - Cold Snap
Albert Collins, Robert Cray & Johnny Copeland – Showdown!
Albert King – Born Under A Bad Sign
Arthur 'Big Boy' Crudup – That's All Right Mama
Bessie Smith – The Complete Recordings, Vol. 1
Big Bill Broonzy – Trouble In Mind
Billie Holiday –Songs for Distingué Lovers
Blind Willie McTell – The Definitive Blind Willie McTell
Bo Diddley – Bo Diddley Is a Gunslinger
Buddy Guy & Junior Wells – Buddy Guy & Junior Wells Play The Blues
Bukka White – The Complete Bukka White
Charley Patton – Pony Blues
Elmore James – Shake Your Moneymaker: The Best of The Fire Sessions
Etta James – The Chess Box
Furry Lewis – Shake 'Em On Down
Gary Moore - Blues for Greeny
Howlin' Wolf – The Chess Box
Jimi Hendrix - Are You Experienced
Jimmy Reed – Blues Masters: The Very Best Of
Joe Bonamassa - Live from the Albert Hall
John Lee Hooker – Alternative Boogie: Early Studio Recordings 1948 – 1952
Johnny Winter - Johnny Winter
Leadbelly – King of the 12-String Guitar
Lightnin' Hopkins – The Complete Prestige/Bluesville Recordings
Lightnin' Slim – Rooster Blues
Lonnie Johnson – The Complete Folkways Recordings
Magic Sam – West Side Soul
Mance Lipscomb – Texas Sharecropper & Songster
Memphis Minnie – The Essential Memphis Minnie
Mississippi John Hurt – 1928 Sessions
Muddy Waters – At Newport 1960
Otis Rush – Cobra Recordings: 1956-1958
Pink Anderson – Ballad and Folksinger – Vol. 3
R.L. Burnside – Wish I Was in Heaven Sitting Down
Reverend Gary Davis – Harlem Street Singer
Robben Ford - Talk to your Daughter & Worried Life Blues
Robert Johnson – King Of the Delta Blues Singers
Skip James – The Complete Early Recordings Of Skip James – 1930
Smoky Babe – Hottest Brand Goin'
Son House – Father Of The Delta Blues: The Complete 1965 Recordings
Sonny Boy Williamson [II] – One Way Out
Stevie Ray Vaughan - Texas Flood & Couldn't Stand the Weather
T-Bone Walker - I Get So Weary
T-Bone Walker – The Complete Imperial Recordings: 1950-1954

Tommy Johnson – Canned Heat (1928-1929)
Willie Dixon – I am The Blues

There really are just too many great blues albums to mention so here's a list of the essential blues guitarists you should check out:

- Albert King
- B.B. King
- Big Bill Broonzy
- Blind William Jefferson
- Bonnie Raitt
- Buddy Guy
- Chris Duarte
- David Gilmour
- Duane Allman
- Eric Clapton
- Freddie King
- Gary Moore
- Jack White
- Jeff Healey
- Jimi Hendrix
- Jimmy Page
- Joe Bonamassa
- John Lee Hooker
- John Mayer
- Johnny Winter
- Jonny Lang
- Kenny Wayne Shepherd
- Lead Belly
- Lightnin' Hopkins
- Luther Allison
- Muddy Waters
- Otis Rush
- Peter Green
- Robben Ford
- Robert Cray
- Robert Johnson
- Rory Gallagher
- Roy Buchanan
- Sonny Landreth
- Stevie Ray Vaughan
- Sue Foley
- T-Bone Walker
- Wes Montgomery

I'm sure I haven't included everyone's favourites so apologies in advance!

Other Books from Fundamental Changes